Eight Keys to Unlock Business Success

... *Even in a Recession*

by

Rob Goddard

DISCLAIMER

Dedication

This book is dedicated to all the wonderful people that I've met on my life's journey so far, who have afforded me their precious time so that I could learn.

In particular, Philip de Lisle, Alex Petty, Andrew Pennington, Tracey Miller and George Swift ...

... and not forgetting my partner in life, Kristina Dine!

I've successfully navigated the start-up, scale up and selling up journey myself. So that from my own personal experiences, I provide insight, guidance & input to other business owners who are currently on that journey themselves. This means that their business grows in a sustainable way, creating increased value over time.

I plan to have a second edition to this book and to include further authors to be an inspiration to others.

So, if you would like to contribute a chapter from your own experiences, do email me on rob.goddard@robgoddard.co.uk

Contents

FOREWARD

This book is intended to help any business owner who is finding the going hard - really hard! It can also apply to someone who may have been redundant and now hankers for setting up their own business for the first time in their life.

Starting and scaling up is hard and it often takes much longer than anticipated to build a sustainable business. This book is a compilation of more than a century's worth of commercial experience from a variety of people in different industries and countries.

It can be lonely at the top, so to learn from others that have been there and have worn the T-shirt is invaluable - not only in terms of knowledge but also experience. These are entrepreneurs who sometimes find running their own business overwhelming, all-demanding and that, occasionally, there seems to be no light at the end of the tunnel.

The following various stories from fellow business owners are honest and candid accounts of what has worked and what hasn't worked during what has been unexpected global turmoil. No country has been left untouched.

A worldwide pandemic which has had a dramatic impact on trade and personal freedoms is one thing, but the lasting impact will be a worldwide recession that will follow, especially as fiscal stimuli from governments around the globe start to be withdrawn.

However, now is the time to go on the front foot, steal a march on your competition and triumph over adversity, rather than to be resigned to your being a victim of it.

From our surveying many other businesses, we have discovered that there are eight keys that lead to success for any business, in any industry and in any country.

This book will share those eight keys to success with you, so that you are better equipped for the journey ahead.

This is not a book on how to get rich quick. Instead, it centres around how to dig deep, persevere, build your self-esteem and inner confidence, so that you can build a robust and sustainable business for the future.

Let me tell you a bit of my own story …

A Bit of My Own Story

by Rob Goddard

Founder and Executive Chairman of Rob Goddard Ltd. Ensuring business owners secure their dream exit by achieving their "magic number" and so open up a new chapter in their lives.
Hampshire, United Kingdom

Some time ago, I travelled up to the 163rd floor of Dubai's 'Burj Khalifa' with the intent of throwing myself off the top of it. Thirteen seconds from certain death to put an end to my depression, guilt and pain.

Half a mile up in the air, looking down to the ground below seemed so surreal. People, cars, trucks and the monorail were like tiny ants scurrying down below. We really are so small compared with the vastness of the land we occupy. The surreal nature of the vista below helped in a strange way. I was detached from 'normal' life. Somehow divorced from it.

I had read on the internet that I would probably die long before I hit the ground because of a cardiac arrest. It also had the added benefit of no repatriation costs. After all, there wouldn't be much of me left to collect.

This all sounds rather macabre, but when you're in a severely depressed state of mind logic and rational thinking take a back seat. It's more about finishing the pain, anguish, anxiety and the utter turmoil of life once and for all.

This was back in 2010, after my having suffered from depression and suicidal thoughts for eighteen months. I was bumping along the bottom of life, trying to scratch a living. We were in the early stages of the last global recession, and I had lost my job, my marriage and relationship with my children in late 2008. I had become self-employed owing to circumstances of life being thrust upon me, rather than a choice or part of some strategic career plan. Not an ideal start to a new business!

When I was employed, I was in the top one per cent of earners in the country and so the fall from grace was immense. I had lost my reason for being - my reason to get up in the morning, my purpose in life.

It's not until you lose something that you realise what you once had. I had taken things and people for granted and, even though I was a big earner, I had also racked up eye-watering debts.

When I lost my job, my world was turned upside down. An abyss opened up in front of me and I had a continual pain in my stomach. Most mornings, I would throw up in the sink before I started the day. Depression to me was like an enormous cloud, moving around as it wished, blocking out light and creating darkness.

I tried to find another job on a six-figure salary, but my applications and interviews proved fruitless. I kept being told, "We like you Rob and we're sure you'd be a valued member of the team, but you're too experienced".

I took that as code for, "You're just too expensive and someone younger would do it for less."

I was forty-five years old at the time and felt like I was on the scrapheap of commercial life. I was supposed to be at the peak of my business career, instead I was at the very bottom.

After eighteen months of my applying for hundreds of jobs and getting absolutely nowhere, a consortium of private investors approached me and said that they were looking to set up a new business venture, and would I like to run it? A very modest salary and a five per cent shareholding.

Wow - a salary! I'd forgotten what one of those was like - and also, I'd be a shareholder for the first time in my life too. It was an easy decision, I had nothing to lose. When you have nothing to lose, decisions are far more straightforward.

In early 2011, I moved gratefully from doing ad-hoc consultancy to a 'proper company' with financial backers.

I will also be grateful to my seed investors, who gave me a another chance in life.

Don't get me wrong, this wasn't a philanthropic move on their part; they were doing it for commercial motives. Unbeknown to me, a number of them had been aware of what I had achieved in the industry and when I made an unsolicited approach to them, they jumped at the chance.

It took eighteen months and over seven hundred submitted CVs to find the right business partner. The lesson I learnt was that perseverance is a key to success. Getting despondent and giving up when things get a bit tough can often rob us of the success that is just around the corner. I've learnt to keep doing the things that you know have worked well in the past. You might need to refine or tweak them over time, but the fundamentals of good business are universal.

Success will surely follow, but it's far more a question of timing. This is why 'get rich quick' schemes don't work. Something of value is earned over time, not in an instant. We can achieve anything; we just can't have everything. The key is not to give up.

My good friend, Dr Andrea Pennington, once said to me, "Resilience is like a muscle. Every time you exercise it, it gets just gets that little bit stronger."

Andrea is spot on. Life's experiences strengthen us. Even the things that don't work out are lessons for us. I've learnt far more from my failures in life than I have from the successes.

I will always be grateful to those original seed investors for backing me and believing in me when I was at the darkest period of my life. Not that they knew at the time, but their involvement at that point in my life was the lifeline that I needed.

Whilst my depression wasn't 'cured' – that took several years more - it gave me hope, a distant light at the end of a long tunnel. When there is no hope, you feel 'hope less'.

Conversely, when you have some hope for better times ahead, it buoys you up. Success moments, no matter how small, keep us going. Little reassurances that we are doing okay, and these should be celebrated as they crop up. With the busyness of life, it's easy to overlook the mini successes. It's good to be in the present, not always striving for something in the future.

I'd like to be able to say, at this point, that I went on to meteoric success in my first business venture, but I didn't.

Even with financial backing with this start up, it was still extremely hard work. We were the 'new kids on the block' and it took considerable time to become established and to build credibility in the marketplace. Earlier, I had worked in the same industry for seven years with another company as General Manager and had steered that company from £1.5m turnover to over £15m.

In effect, I had served my apprenticeship in the Mergers and Acquisitions industry. However, I had done that as an employee. Moreover, this business itself had many years successful trading behind it before I joined it. I just took it to the next level of success.

The situation I now found myself in was a very different prospect. Getting a start-up business up and running is akin to pulling or pushing a car. It feels like a dead weight at the outset and takes immense strength to get the wheels moving and build up enough momentum. It's exhausting. When I invest now, I avoid start-ups because the amount of equity offered is not in keeping with the risk and effort required. Instead, I have a preference for mature businesses. Less of an equity share, yes - but far less risk and effort.

In my experience, start-ups are the most difficult things to make work successfully. Twenty per cent never get beyond Year One and forty per cent never see their fifth birthday. It requires tenacity, self-belief and the ability to close deals. A lack of cashflow in the early years hampers the majority of early-stage companies.

Then there is the emotional toll. I can recall during those formative years, pulling up in my fifteen-year-old rusty Audi A4, parking round the corner from a prospect's office, just crying out the pure emotion. The combination of doubt, depression, and trying to make ends meet was overwhelming at times.

I'd have a good cry in the car, wipe my eyes and nose with tissues, then brace myself to go into the next sales pitch. I remember looking at my eyes in the rear-view mirror, making sure that they weren't too red before I went inside.

In one sense, it was the old adage of 'fake it till you make it' idea. I felt unworthy of my being in front of people selling to them, because my personal life was in the toilet.

However, it started to work. I was starting to get traction with new sales. My self-esteem was gradually repairing with each new order. People were trusting me to sell their businesses and deep down it felt really good.

Within months, I made my first hire, Kay. There's always a nervousness about your first hire, because it immediately reduced your profit. Then you have concerns about its not working out, maybe having to let someone go, etc.

I need not have worried: Kay was excellent. She was highly experienced and could turn her hand to anything - administration, marketing or research. She was a breath of fresh air and is still with the business today. The best bit, though, about hiring her was it was Kay and me against the world. Mutual support and lots of laughter each week. Someone to bounce ideas off. It was so therapeutic to team up with another individual and to tackle the task ahead, together.

In the ensuing twelve months, I employed several other people. We had a cohesive team, aligned in what we wanted to achieve. The other added benefit was that I didn't have the need to spend money with any recruitment agencies. All my hires were people that worked for me before, or people that had been referred by an existing member of staff.

Think of it: growing a team of six people, without having to pay any agencies to recruit them. Also, you know what you're buying, warts and all, if you have worked with someone before. If they have come from an internal staff referral, they are going to be very suitable. Existing staff members wouldn't put anyone forward for a job if they didn't feel it would be a good fit.

With a small team of motivated people, I no longer felt alone and exposed. I was leading a handpicked team, receiving a salary and I was a shareholder! What a change in fortune. It wasn't the end destination for me, but I did feel I was coming out of the other side.

This is the upside of starting a business from scratch. You give birth to it, nurture it and see it grow. Being a founder of business is like being a parent: it may not be the perfect child but you're very proud of it. You're creating something of value from nothing.

The hard part comes when you want to sell your business. It's like selling your child. It's part of you, part of your identity. Letting go is just as hard as getting the thing started in the first place. There is a process to follow and I go through this in my many videos on the subject of selling up.

It took several years to break through the £500k annual sales threshold and, by doing so, we entered an exclusive club. Did you know that only three per cent of businesses turnover more than £500k a year? Nor did I, until I started doing some research.

The shape of business demographics is like a port decanter: very thin at the top, but with a very big bottom. There are over five million small businesses in this country and only a few hundred thousand larger businesses. Napoleon was right: we are an island of shopkeepers. In fact, having worked in the US, Middle East and mainland Europe, I can say that it's true all over. It must be something to do with the human condition. To be innovative and want to create a future for ourselves.

Back to my own business growth journey. Once we exceeded £500k in sales, we weren't going to let it stay there. We wanted to push on and break through the 'magic million'. We achieved that in Year Six, and what was instrumental in that growth step was the recruiting of Steve, the year before.

Steve and I had worked together for many years in a previous life, and he was my role model for all things sales. He was confident, charismatic and an impressive closer of deals. He was my early role model in sales and I worked for him for ten years. A really inspirational guy.

Years later, in his late fifties, he was made redundant and was vigorously trying to find re-employment, but without success. Ironically, it reminded me of my own struggles years before. We often think that our trial and tribulations in life are somehow just for us. Singled out for special treatment. Of course, the reality is true. Adversity is faced by most of us. What varies is the way we respond to it.

Our employing Steve catapulted the business into another performance bracket, and it went on to becoming a multi-million-pound company. I could not have achieved this without recruiting a salesperson that was even better than me! .

So, another key for success is to employ or engage people that are better than you at certain tasks. Some business owners struggle with this, mistakenly thinking that they need to be King or Queen of the hill - a legend in their own lunchtime.

The reverse is true: for it to be able to scale up sustainably, the business needs the team to deliver the results, not the owner.

If the owner is at the centre of everything, it's self-limiting for the business and causes undue stress and pressure on the owner. Sacrifices are often made, especially with the family. I know that was true in my case. I lost so much time of my children's growing up because I was working. My life lacked balance.

Taking the laptop on holiday, crack of dawn starts, late night return from yet another networking event in London ... I have fallen foul of all of these, and many more. It's the overwhelming pressure of needing to keep up, especially if the business is growing fast. Often, we can neglect other things in our lives that are equally as important - arguably more so.

Despite this success, I still had a nagging doubt in my mind: would it all collapse one day in a heap?

Twice I had built a career, only to lose it and start from the bottom again. Just like the game of "Snakes and Ladders", you make steady progress, then in an instant you find yourself cascading down the 'snakes' and ending up back on square one.

I used to have recurrent and disturbing dreams that I was on a plane and as we were climbing in altitude someone would stand up, automatic gun in hand and bring the plane down. An assassin on the plane. These were my subconscious fears that whatever had been built was only temporary and that a force stronger than me would bring it all crashing down.

Apart from death and taxation, nothing in Life is guaranteed. However, I've learnt to adapt my mindset. It's possible that I could lose it all tomorrow, but I'm now far better equipped to handle it, if that ever happened.

My starting point is to ask myself, "What's the worst that can happen?" Originally, it was buying a second-hand transit van - white of course - and go and do house clearances, then sell items on E-Bay and car boot events.

And if I had no permanent abode, I could convert the van and sleep in it!

The other strategy I used was to invest far more time in friendships and family. Having a network of people around you that care and are supportive is essential. People who care about you as person, not what you are in life, or what you have achieved.

Nowadays, if I lost it all, the worst that can happen is that we would move to Albania and live in our beachfront property. My pensions and investments would stretch four times further, too. Debt free, mortgage free. I could retire early.

Not that I would; I already have an Albanian travel business, helping tourists discover the hidden gem in Europe with excursions, boat charters and holiday lets.

Ultimately, none of us can control Life's events but we can refashion our mindset in order to cope when something hits us square in the face.

With Steve onboard, leading the sales drive, bringing in new clients, my attention focused on my returning to Dubai and setting up a similar business over there, using the blueprint of the successful UK business.

I went to live and work in Dubai in 2010 to run away from my problems and debts in the UK. Starting with a fresh canvas where nobody knew me, I could start again.

The trouble was, in doing so, I had cut myself off from my support network whilst battling with depression. Also, the job was commission only - real hardcore stuff.

That's why, after several months, I made the decision one day to end it all, go to the Burj Khalifa and find a way to jump from it. If you want to discover why I'm still here to tell the tale, you'll need to read my book, "Suicide to Success: How a Locked Exit Gave Me a Way Out" (Rob Goddard Books, 2019).

Returning to the UAE was more than my replicating a successful business model from the UK in another country. For me, it was about facing my demons. I had failed out there six years before and I wanted to go back and make it a commercial success the second time around. If I didn't, it would always be a time in my life that I'd regret. Failed to make work.

I wanted to slay that dragon in my life. Nothing to do with Dubai itself, it's a wonderful place, brimming with opportunity. The problem was within me.

At the same time of my venturing back to Dubai, I bought out my original seed investors and simultaneously brought in three new investors. There are often seasons for people to work together. I was finding with my original investors that our plans for the future were diverging.

It was time to change things around. Shareholders and investors must be aligned about direction and overall strategy. Failure to do so can cause division, ill-feeling and, eventually, adversely affect the performance of the very business that they own.

The new investors have been excellent. They have afforded me the space to grow the business and experiment with new ideas. Also, having a sounding board of different individuals for a common aim is very healthy. In fact, I would say it's essential.

The next big step in the growth of my business was to appoint my successor in 2018, a chap called Mike. Again, Mike and I successfully worked many years ago and so I trusted him. Trust is huge if you are passing over your 'baby' to someone else to run day to day.

This is immensely hard, and many owners fail to achieve this transition and find themselves locked in a self-made prison. Maybe a golden prison, because they are taking a good income from their business, but nevertheless they can feel trapped by the very thing they created.

Some then try to sell their business on to someone else and soon find that an owner-reliant business is largely unsaleable. Too many businesses are largely reliant on their owners. This is a mistake and adversely affects the value of their business when they come to sell it.

The enlightened strategy is to have a succession plan. Which is what I did. For a while Mike and I worked alongside each other. He was learning the ropes in a new industry, and I started to find some time was opening up in my diary.

We could only afford to employ Mike because of the step change growth that Steve had initiated a couple of years previously. We even had ten months' cash buffer in the business, so now was a perfect time to recruit my replacement.

Once Mike came on board, I started to find I had time for other things. I became involved with a local cancer charity and a benefactor of an Albanian orphanage. To be able to give back to others is immensely satisfying and takes the focus away from the ups and downs of your own life. We can get so entrenched in our own issues that we lose sight of the needs of others. It can put our own troubles into perspective.

I was also being approached by business owners for mentoring and coaching. I had always resisted it because I was already working seventy to ninety hours a week, but now I had more bandwidth with Mike running up to speed as my successor.

What I absolutely love about helping fellow business owners on their journey is when the penny drops for them - they make a change, and they see an improvement.

It's that same sense of pride I have had with my children, learning to ride a bike, passing their driving test or gaining a degree at university.

It was last year that it dawned on me that I could go one step further, dilute my shareholding, take some cash off the table and not be involved in the operational side of the business at all.

After twenty years in the sector and my spending the past decade scaling my business, I was looking for fresh challenges and new experiences.

Enjoying your work is one of the fundamental elements of a contented life. I still wanted to be associated with the business, but I didn't want to run it anymore. So, I reduced my shareholding to a modest amount and stepped down from the business – without entirely stepping out of it.

I am an 'Ambassador' of the business, working with business owners and helping them prepare their own business - and themselves - for an eventual exit. It's so rewarding helping others to find their own exit, as I have done myself.

I also now choose who I work with and when. This is true freedom. Ironically, I have gone full circle and become a solopreneur once more. It's taken thirteen years, but I'm back where I started. I wonder whether that's why they call it the "Circle of Life"?

However, Life is very different now, as is the way I look at it. I always have a contingency in the back of my mind. I always weigh up the cost of taking certain actions.

Also, my sense of self-worth is not rooted in what I have or don't have. Rather, it's based on my having fun with the people that matter most to me and enjoying good health.

When you boil it down, the only things that really matter in Life are the relationships we have and not being ill. Money is a short term motivator: it doesn't bring contentment. I know many wealthy people who are unhappy, anxious and lacking in purpose.

All of us face adversity in our lives. There's a challenge ahead, even financial turmoil sometimes. What matters is our being open to change and having the courage to move forward. This is made easier when we benefit from the support of others around us.

My other half, Kristina, would say I'm a stubborn individual. I tell her I like to think of myself as single-minded and focused! It depends which way you look at it.

Successful business owners are a very rare breed, in my experience. That's why most people on this planet are employees. Successful business owners often like to make their own rules rather than follow the rules of others. We want to beat the system and have a sense of our achieving something of long-term value.

That can often mean our leaving a legacy that we're proud of - something that will stand the test of time. However, I want to create a 'living legacy'. After all, what's the point of leaving things behind after you're dead? Where's the fun in that?

To find out more: rob.goddard@robgoddard.co.uk

www.robgoddard.co.uk

KEY 1: COMMITMENT

When problems come along and threaten your business, disrupting your flow and causing you anxiety and worry, it can be hard to remember why you started this venture in the first place.

I don't think there's an entrepreneur alive who hasn't wondered, "What on earth was I thinking starting this nightmare?" at some point.

That's where Key 1 comes in: your commitment to your goal and your path needs to be rock solid from Day One so that you continue towards your success.

Commitment is not tenacity. If tenacity is 'hanging in there' through gritting your teeth, then commitment is your decision to achieve your goal.

The Romans had it right (as with many things) when they came up with the verb in Latin on which 'decision' is based.

"Decire: to cut off"

To make a decision about your goal is to cut yourself off from any other eventuality. This is an outright commitment to one result.

Many people like to commit to a single path to achieve the goal, too, but I think that can undermine your success. There may be several paths worth trying in order to achieve it, so rather commit to the end result and keep an open mind about how you get there.

Your business's core values need commitment, too. There's no point in having them if nobody heeds them. Again, though, it's a misconception to think that they have to be written in stone and obeyed forever. In reality, colleagues, partners and staff will come and go over the years and the group dynamic will change every time. Hopefully, you'll be careful to choose people with the same personal values as you, so the core values won't have to change radically … but keep in mind that you need to allow growth in the core values as your business grows and develops.

After a horrible time of illness during which John couldn't work, he found it impossible to get back into the job market. He started his business feeling on the backfoot, but with the support of his lovely life partner and undiluted commitment, he designed and brought his business to life. This next story demonstrates how you can achieve your goal when you single-mindedly chase it down.

Tubthumping

by John Surgenor

Owner, Barrington Hamilton Personal Asset Management
London, United Kingdom

Lee, my second wife, is my rock. We have been married for a few days over three years. She loves adventures and travelling, especially to hot destinations where there is an abundant supply of cocktails.

Lee didn't sign up for what I am about to share with you. Nobody does in these situations. For better for worse, eh? She has certainly had to deal with "for worse" and, later, she would admit to friends that I had milked that particular vow.

Today is January 7th 2010.

It's dark outside as the alarm beeps its monotonous high tone that Lee absolutely hates. I didn't sleep well. Lee confirmed she didn't either. It's always like this when we have to travel the twenty-five or so miles for my three-weekly chemotherapy cycle.

A 'chemo day' starts at 6.30am when the alarm sounds; a quick hot shower, perhaps a little breakfast and we're in the car at 7am as we're expected in the Guildford Oncology Unit at 8am.

Although I'm feeling really crap today, I always look forward to seeing the nursing team; they're great. I really like Sarah - John, too. Sarah is lovely and so, so caring. She is a busy mum and somehow fits working in the Oncology Unit around family responsibilities. I'm in awe – she deserves a medal. John lives for his holidays often in the Philippines with his partner. As he regales us with details of his most recent trip, Lee makes a couple of notes on her iPhone as to possible future holiday destinations.

John's so sweet; he always rubs his hands and my arm when it's cold before finding the vein that will be the temporary gateway into my bloodstream for the three different poisons that drip, drip, drip into me all day. It's a long day for all involved. For the first hour and the last hour of the day until around 6pm, they simply flush my system with saline solution.

Today will be different.

I really don't feel well when I get up. I should still be on a high, as just four days ago Jermaine Beckford scored the winner at Old Trafford in the third round of the FA Cup! I've followed Leeds United ever since I lived in Wetherby as a young boy. I didn't really appreciate it at that time but virtually all of my school friends at Wetherby County Primary supported Leeds.

I struggle into the shower. Drying myself and getting dressed saps my strength. Today, the towel seems so heavy and drying myself is an enormous effort. I weigh just over ten stone. My fighting weight in healthier times was over fourteen stone. You do the maths.

When I get downstairs, Lee gives her usual command. "You must eat something. It's going to be a long day."

"I'm really not hungry".

"Try," she implores. "Please".

I shake out just half a bowl of Rice Krispies, pour on the cold milk and eventually manage to down most of it. Lee has already started warming the car up. Her black Audi Q5 is her pride and joy. The heated seats are a real bonus on a typical cold morning in January.

We reach the outskirts of Horsham and I can't I stop myself.

"Please stop the car!" I blurt out. "I feel sick".

She immediately pulls over. I tumble out and retch up the few Rice Krispies I've eaten. Then, we continue the journey to Guildford in silence.

At 8am, Lee explains to Sarah that I've been sick on the way in as she starts me on the saline drip and takes my bloods. I drift away in thought, hiding the turmoil of my emotions. How did I get here? Why me?

In time, I would realise it isn't just me. Thousands of people are impacted every year by a shock diagnosis. And boy, is it a shock! It's not just the patient that's impacted. The partner, of course, and all of the extended family are impacted. It's just hideous.

After an hour my oncologist, Seb, asks to see me. I always find it odd shuffling along pushing a kind of coat stand on wheels around the oncology ward with various wires inserted into my body wearing one of those thin drab gowns.

Seb is very concerned by my sickness and general weakness and decides that I am just not strong enough to take the poison that day. We sit in silence for a few moments. I then ask the question I have been wanting to ask for some weeks. I know Lee doesn't want me to ask it.

"How long have I got, Doctor, seriously"?

Citing the usual evasive caveats at first, he tells me directly.

"The average for this kind of cancer is around five years, but for you I think we are looking at two years at the most. I'm sorry".

Lee and I slowly trudge back to the small room where Sarah, in tears after Lee explains what Seb has said, carefully removes the IV catheter so we can go back to our place and try and comprehend the enormity of Seb's words.

Just four months earlier in September 2009 I had Mr Worthington's diagnosis of cancer: there was a neuroendocrine tumour in my small intestine.

No, funnily enough I had not heard of that term 'neuroendocrine' before. He didn't seem too happy when I asked whether it was serious. 'Neuroendocrine' was to become a very common term in our lexicon.

Before the bombshell Lee and I were enjoying life. We had experienced some terrific holidays together; Maldives, Las Vegas, Hong Kong to name a few.

In February of that year came a milestone. I started my own independent financial advice company, Barrington Hamilton Personal Asset Management. It was something I wanted to do, but do differently, ethically and not just to copy the fairly prevalent product-selling outfits that heavily populated the profession.

I didn't really have any clients, just two or three who I had advised with a previous authorised hat on. My main income at that time came from a self-employed marketing business I had founded a few years earlier, one that brought innovative offerings for financial advisers to use with their clients. But the plan was always to start and build Barrington Hamilton from scratch to eventually replace my self-employed income.

An acquaintance at that time who was in PR advised me not to use the word "Private" in the title of my fledgling business and use "Personal" instead. Too many firms were already using "Private". Too common, he said. He also advised me not to use my surname in the title. Just imagine "Surgenor Personal Wealth" or some such! The lightbulb moment came when I learned his middle name – Barrington. My middle name is Hamilton. Thousands were therefore not spent on consultants.

In March 2009, Lee convinced me I should book an appointment with the GP.

"Why?" I exclaimed. "I feel just fine."

"You are continuing to lose weight and I'm worried," she responded. I pointed out that I had been losing weight since leaving my employed role in London a few years earlier. Those days were filled with a plethora of corporate lunches, dinners and beers with the team. Of course I was losing weight! I wasn't enjoying those unhealthy activities any more.

Reluctantly, I went to see my GP, Ed. We liked Ed - knowledgeable, approachable and friendly Ed. He listened to my description of the minor symptoms I had been experiencing. Nothing that didn't affect all men of a certain age, I thought. Tummy troubles.

He referred me to a specialist at Gatwick Spire to be on the safe side. Endoscopy, colonoscopy, endless blood tests and another endoscopy. Five months of check-ups. Five months of seemingly endless check-ups.

It was becoming tiresome!

I was further referred to Guildford, to a Mr Worthington, who unbeknown to me at that point was to become the absolute superhero in my life. I remember cheekily parking in the Best Practice Head Office car park one September afternoon in Horsham. Who doesn't like free parking? Dayna was in the car park having a cigarette and asked where I was going. I explained yet another test, one using an ultrasonic endoscope, technology not then available at Gatwick. I was leaving the car there, catching a train and Lee, who worked in Guildford, would take us both back home.

Not once - and I genuinely mean not once - did I ever think the problem would be cancer, a relatively rare one at that. It is not a cancer that is the result of risky lifestyle choices, I am told. This one is simply bad luck.

Mr Worthington operated on me inside of two weeks after confirming the diagnosis. It was a Friday, a long operation. Lee told my children from my first marriage, teenagers Sacha and Jamie that I was expected to be out of theatre by 9pm.

Sacha made me laugh. "Oh, no!" she groaned in a very serious manner. "The Tudors is on at 9pm. Can you call after if possible?" Kids. Bless them!

Sadly, this time he was unable to remove the tumour. Chemotherapy beckoned ...

After two years of my not really being physically able to work, I was well enough to get life started again. Mr Worthington had worked wonders in my second operation in January 2011, a full 'Whipples Procedure' that resulted in a five-week stay in hospital. Yes, five weeks! They are termed "complications".

My self-employed income was now close to non-existent. My not working had meant no new business. Existing business was in tatters mainly as a result of the credit crunch. Client monies redeemed. I suppose I could view it as a compliment: my fund offerings were liquid with the underlying client able to redeem, unlike many of the esoteric 'clever' fund offerings at that time.

The alarm sounds at 6.30am on Monday 5th September 2011.

It's my first day back at work. What do I do now? How do I spend it? How do I find a new client?

Today? Tomorrow? How am I going to earn money?

We're running on empty financially with a mortgage to pay and maintenance to my ex-wife. Barrington Hamilton is a limited company; the financials are available for all to see. What do I do now to secure a pay cheque?

I contact a couple of recruitment consultants. I've updated my CV and am uncertain an employed role would suit me but needs must! I'm looking for opportunities to become a Business Development Manager for one of the insurance, pension or investment companies.

The kind of job I left in 2004 to go self-employed. The kind of job I'm good at but came to despise. Not because of the people, I love the people. But the internal politics, the red tape, the feeling of not being in control. Your target rises annually, sometimes by an arbitrarily high percentage. The company can change your deal, your team's deal on a whim, make you redundant on a whim, stop a product line on a whim.

To me, it's a retrograde step, although the regular monthly pay cheque will come in very handy right now.

We were struggling. All along, though, a little voice inside my head was telling me to do something else.

"You started Barrington Hamilton for all of the right reasons, just continue!"

But I had no self-employed income. How would I start? How would this be possible?

"I've not done this before. It's all new to me. Help! I'm frightened," I replied again and again to that little voice.

I also admitted to myself that I felt ashamed. Ashamed because here I was, nearly fifty years old and having to start again. There was little to show for my years working from the age eighteen to forty-nine. My rock deserved more.

The little voice became louder after my conversation with a friendly, open and pragmatic recruitment consultant.

"John, your CV reads well up until you unfortunately became unwell and didn't work for two years. The world has moved on in that time; more and more providers are launching investment platforms. It's the future. Clients will hold pretty much all of their assets on these platforms. You don't have any recent or relevant experience in this space. Prospective employers will expect to see some of this kind of experience. Your age as well is against you. At this time employers are wanting younger BDMs, eager and steely ones who will look to make this a long-term career move".

I was stunned. I thanked him for his honesty. Agism live and kicking! I really didn't think that my age would count against me.

Sometime later I mentally thanked that recruitment consultant. He unwittingly did me a favour. He made my mind up that I had to listen to the little voice and build a financial advice business from scratch.

The little voice was stubborn, determined but also guarded. It urged me not to submit to the working, employed life in which I once excelled. It pleaded with me.

I felt compelled to try. I reminded myself why I was starting again at age forty-nine.

Because I have to. Because I want to.

There were no barriers. I didn't have the security of a regular wage. Lee, still my rock said she would support me whatever I decided to do.

I actually felt blessed to be in this position.

I've learnt that growing a business at any time takes effort, persistence, guile and luck. You need to sow seeds, many seeds, before it starts to bear fruit. But growing a business when there's a recession? You really will need to have planted seeds way in advance or you are likely to have a bleak period and poor harvest.

Do you have a similar little voice in your head that's encouraging you to make that break for your freedom, to go out on your own? Just you versus the world? Then hopefully my story will encourage you and my reason for writing it will have been fulfilled.

I'm told we regret the things we didn't do rather than the things we did that may not have turned out as we hoped for. I want to motivate you if you've not yet made that jump. Perhaps this book should be renamed "How to keep growing a business, even in a recession." Keeping on moving forwards was hugely important to me in those early months and years when activity was high although productivity was low.

"You've got to kiss a lot of frogs," they told me. And they were right!

I was reminded of the fable of "The Chinese Bamboo Tree": you take a little seed, plant it, water it, and fertilise it for a whole year, and nothing happens.

During the second year, you water it and fertilise it … and nothing happens.

The third year you water it and fertilise it, and still nothing happens. How discouraging this becomes!

The fourth year you water it and fertilise it, and again nothing happens. This is very frustrating.

The fifth year you continue to water and fertilise the seed and then …

sometime during the fifth year, the Chinese bamboo tree sprouts and grows a full ninety feet in six weeks!

Building a business is very similar to the growing process of the Chinese bamboo tree. It is often discouraging. We seemingly do things right and nothing happens. But for those who do things right and are not discouraged and are persistent, things will happen. Finally, we begin to receive the rewards. The rewards are not purely financial. Running your own business brings joy, freedom, control and pleasure. Pleasure from achievements of your own making. Hard work, yes, hard work. But very satisfying work.

So, did the Chinese bamboo grow ninety feet over six weeks or five years? I think the latter.

Back to that Monday morning. How did I go about generating new client enquiries? Thinking back, of course, there was an element of luck but I believe you make your own luck through activity. Hey! I was due some luck. Activity is key and so I got moving.

I thought about what I was good at. What had I learned from all of those years at Scottish Equitable? The answer was 'relationship building' - not just person to person but also business to business. In theory, although I had never attempted it before, I should be able to develop relationships with other professionals such as accountants and solicitors.

Surely, though, they all already had business relationships with advisers? Was it a closed shop? There was only one way to find out. I was determined not to go down the route that the new recruits of one or two large national restricted-advice giants are encouraged to go down to find clients: work your friends and family, sell them something … perhaps even a financial product they need.

No thanks.

But why would other professionals refer clients to me? I'm a sole trader, I thought; I don't have the so-called resources of larger firms.

My little voice piped up. "You need to do what a friend of mine, Matt Anderson terms in his timeless classic book Fearless Referrals as 'putting water in the well'," it said. "You need to work out how to help them first. You can't just ask for business 'cold'. It doesn't work."

So how did I help them and put water in their wells?

In various ways. One example was offering in-house training sessions for their teams.

"Who else offers these sessions to you?" I asked.

"Nobody," was the usual reply.

I knew that I was not there just to develop their knowledge; I would be remembered if I also 'entertained'. I made the session informative, interactive and fun. And I made sure that the learning and development was relevant to them. I showed how my expertise could dovetail with theirs, be they accountants, private client lawyers or family lawyers. I looked at case studies where the joined-up expertise improved a client's situation and outcome.

In the meantime, I had been passing my Chartered Insurance Institute exams. I qualified as a Chartered Financial Planner in 2012, one of the earlier cohorts. I was awarded distinctions in the then three major pension exams. I'm not saying that to impress you in any way, but in what area do family lawyers need assistance? Pensions. So, why not deal with someone who has put water in the well and has distinctions in pension exams?

My advice to you is to think about what you can do and what you need to do. If I can do it, then you can as well. All of a sudden, the sole trader has more to offer than the so-called resources of larger firms!

Retrospectively, mentally analysing the whole episode some years later I appreciated it was bizarrely good luck. Without my hitting rock bottom with my health and running on empty financially, would I have embarked on the task of building my own business from scratch? I couldn't go any lower, the only way was up! My cancer experience enabled me to finally see my vocation in life to help others get the most out of their lives, live the lives they want to live without fear of ever running out of money. Life is indeed precious, we're here just for a fleeting moment in time and it is slipping away at incredible speed.

I'm not sure I agree with the phrase "You only live once". I think rather, "You only die once, so live every day."

We have the power to change our lives. Believe you can and you just might.

Here are some highlights of my good fortune – or perhaps, rather, 'activity' - that started me off.

Firstly, over a coffee a friend said he knew a partner at a local law firm and he would mention me to him. Thanks!

We went for lunch. A long lunch which I later learnt was not untypical!

"John, I have very much enjoyed lunch; however, I already have a number of relationships with IFAs," he said.

Not a great start, I thought, and I'm £200 down. Although he was not in a position to help directly, he kindly referred me to his colleague, Reshma, in their private client team.

Reshma then referred me to Melanie in their family team.

Melanie referred me to Stephen, a family lawyer from another law firm.

Reshma then introduced me to Jackie at a local accountancy firm.

My friend Chris introduced me to a pensions actuary, Geoff.

A retired IFA, Keith, on whom I had previously called in London when working for Scottish Equitable then introduced me to Steve and Simon at an accountancy firm with seven offices.

Keith and I had kept in touch and our paths crossed again when he was working in Eastbourne and I was running the Brighton office for Scottish Equitable. I put water in his well as when he retired he had to make his daughter redundant. The hardest thing he had ever had to do workwise he told me. I helped find work for his daughter in a very small way for Barrington Hamilton but mainly through introductions to other financial advisers who were looking for her expertise.

I'm glad to report that Anna is still with me, now our excellent Technical Manager. Every meeting is a chance to impress but more importantly a chance to build relationships. These professionals are the gatekeepers to your ideal clients.

Then, it happened! My phone rang and Geoff, the self-proclaimed World's Greatest Actuary was on the line (he is, by the way.)

"John, it's Geoff here. Got a friend who needs your help. I've been telling him he needs to speak to an independent adviser. Been telling him for months and now he thinks he's not being told the whole truth about his pension and investments. His name's Mario. I'll forward his details".

"I'd love to help Geoff – thanks". And there it was. Mario became my first client and I'm glad to report he still is!

And it continued. I carried on picking up clients. Yes, I admit to my making many mistakes in and on my business. I look back to the early days and cringe at some of the clumsy meetings I had with prospective clients who didn't become clients, funnily enough! I have sat in front of nearly one hundred and sixty people that didn't become clients for one reason or another.

Do make a list of all prospective client meetings and add a short comment as to the outcome. Analysing these records help shape future meetings. I use a simple 'traffic lights' system overview on my prospects spreadsheet: red, amber or green. Year after year. Despite setbacks, you just keep going.

The catalyst for a deluge of new clients was the fastest stock market fall in history that commenced in this recession in early 2020 – the pandemic recession. My best year ever!

Seeds planted in previous years were bearing fruit. A record harvest of referred clients since starting my business, and in a recession! You might recall the panic that investors felt especially when unnecessarily stirred up by so called financial journalists in March 2020 with headlines like these:

- Pandemic crashes global stock markets

- It's a rout on global stock markets, not far off crash territory

- The FTSE 100 has just had its worst day since Black Monday in October 1987

- Complacency to chaos: how COVID-19 sent the world's markets into freefall

- Stock markets in biggest fall since 2008 as virus fears trigger panic selling

An initial paragraph read: "For the global financial system, it has been a month of unprecedented pandemonium as the coronavirus pandemic breaks all records, bringing western capitalism to its knees as the disease spreads."

What a load of tosh! I received a text asking whether I would be willing to speak to someone who wasn't happy with his current (restricted) advisers. Of course! I called GP, an ex-professional footballer, and asked him to explain what the issues were.

"John, I have not received any contact from my adviser during these worrying times with the markets. No calls, no emails. I have left a couple of messages but I've not heard anything."

"Oh, that's not ideal," I remarked. I went on to explain that although arguably overdue, it is common for global stock markets to depreciate in value, but that they always recover. The thing to do is nothing. Don't make the big mistake of selling to cash, don't fiddle with your portfolio, just ride it out. This too shall pass.

He seemed reassured especially after I forwarded the four emails I had already sent to existing clients to reassure them. My first new client of the recession! GP referred his father, then another ex-footballer he'd roomed with. Then another.

Prior to the stock market falls in early 2020, I formed a habit at annual planning meetings with clients whereby I would always say something like, "We've been lucky as investors since March 2009. The stock markets have been going one way post Credit Crunch, and that's up! At some point our luck will change and the reverse will happen but only on a temporary basis. Declines are always temporary in nature. The long-term upward trend is permanent".

I would hold a kind of lifeboat drill to prepare clients for when our luck changed and explored with them their likely emotions and reactions if they saw their £1m+ savings fall by 30%, for argument's sake.

"How would you feel?"

"How would you react?"

Of course, these dry runs were fine but we had to wait for the acid test of the sudden global stock market falls caused by investor panic due to COVID-19. I'm delighted to report that not a single client panicked and switched their investments to cash. One had to be talked in off the ledge though!

I still think myself fortunate as opposed to my being some marketing guru. I'm just me.

I was lucky because I had sown seeds when times were very testing, testing because of ill health. I had to start from scratch at the age of forty-nine after two years of being too poorly to work. I was lucky because I have met some inspirational peers who were only too willing to pass on their experience and knowledge of growing a business. Special mentions to Andy Hart and your authoritative 'uncle', Nick Lincoln.

There are also some great writers and professionals that provide knowledge in books and seminars. I sniffed out these resources.

You have to decide what kind of adviser you want to be then go out and learn the knowledge that will take you there. Nothing happens until you do something. I was fortunate as I was forced to do something! We have the power to alter the course of our lives. Courage, conviction and a strong purpose.

I have built a successful business from scratch because I had to. Anecdotally, there are adviser practices that have struggled to attract new clients or only a trickle of new clients during this recession. It's not that they were doing anything fundamentally wrong during the pandemic; rather, it perhaps points to their not doing the right things beforehand in the lead up to the pandemic.

My business onboarded more ideal clients during the COVID-19 pandemic's twelve-month period than at any other time since being in existence. Many of these already had an adviser but were exasperated at the lack of communication. The recession to date has yielded over twenty-five new clients. This company year is forecasted to show an increase of over 40% in repeat ongoing fees over the previous year. This must be the equivalent of my Chinese bamboo tree growing ninety feet in six weeks!

So, am I cancer-free? Yes, I'm pleased to report. There are still some health issues though after such a large operation now ten years ago. But I'm relaxed about them. I'm part of a post-Whipples research study at the Royal Surrey in Guildford: 'Long term consequences of pancreatic resection'. That's me! Surviving ten years plus is sadly not the norm. It depends on how your cancer presented.

It's 11.30pm on 6th August 2020. My rock has called an ambulance. She's also called her eighty-five year-old Mum to look after our two Jack-a-poos. She has to collect her Mum to bring her over to our home. My rock is now rushing to East Surrey Hospital. She telephones my daughter Sacha. Tears from both.

"Sacha, can you let Jamie (my son) know?"

It's now one o'clock in the morning. My rock fears the worst.

Sepsis. Again.

This time is scarier for her as I am unresponsive when led to the ambulance. Dimly, I'm aware of my being asked to descend the stairs on my backside. I'm very unwell.

My rock parks at the hospital and rushes in.

"You can't see him," she's told. "He's still unresponsive".

The sepsis was caused by a bile leak. I was operated on again. A revision of hepaticojejunostomy and gastroenterostomy! Mr Worthington worked wonders and cleared the blockage just south of my liver. Dr Hatrick treated the most recent episode of sepsis and cholangitis by performing a Percutaneous transhepatic cholangiography (PTC) procedure. I admit to this not being a comfortable experience, as skilful as Dr Hatrick is!

Put your trust in the medical experts. They literally work wonders. None of us knows how long we have on this wonderful planet.

I feel better now. Onwards.

Now, I need to decide whether to take the plunge and hire another adviser ... but that's the next chapter.

With thanks to:

Mr Tim Worthington, Consultant Surgeon at the Royal Surrey County Hospital

Dr Sebastian Cummins, Consultant Clinical Oncologist, St Luke's Cancer Centre, Royal Surrey County Hospital

Dr Andrew Hatrick, Consultant Interventional Radiologist at Frimley Park Hospital NHS Foundation Trust

To find out more: john@barringtonhamilton.co.uk

www.barringtonhamilton.co.uk

KEY 2: VALUES

What is it about some people that makes them a total headache to work with? Why can't everybody be born with a set of social rules that is universally acknowledged and practiced? Dogs have a code of conduct that they practice with each other; why do we have to be so complicated?

You know the kind of person I'm talking about. The client who demands too much, who barks orders, who underpays or moans about your fee. The type of colleague who takes the credit for your work or undermines your expertise.

Hopefully, you're already in the position where you don't have to bother with those types financially. If you're not, though, learning to manage these people and even saying 'no' is a rough ride that all of we entrepreneurs need to take at some stage.

What those tricky types don't understand is that a business person's most valuable asset is their reputation. They can have all the money in the world, the biggest fleet of vehicles or thousands of employees, but if their reputation is bad then others will not want to work with them.

One of the things that we need to develop as early as possible in our business running journey is respect – for self and for others. Without it, we can't hope to grow in the following, vital ways:

- Partnership: as we'll see, our support systems and networks are central to our wellbeing and our businesses' growth. If you're at the happy stage of recruiting someone to join your team, look for someone with the right set of intrinsic values. They won't be able to change them once they join you.

- Integrity: honesty and fairness in all things can be difficult to maintain when you're challenged but keep it you must. Your reputation is on show – and it's your greatest asset, remember.

- Moral code: if you choose to work with people who have similar ethics to you, you're unlikely to run into trouble. A shared, solid code of ethics does wonders for building trust between people. What are yours? Do you have your values written down, ready to share with someone you might want to work with one day?

- Trust: do others feel that they can trust you when they meet you? Do you know of someone that you don't trust? They might make you feel edgy, insecure and defensive – all very apt instinctive warning signs that you should keep your distance. If one party breaks another's trust, that relationship is over.

My friend Alex has played an important role in my life. In his early years of practicing personal development and business coaching, he took on some clients that he would rather have done without. We've all been there …

In this next story, he shares how he shaped his values and chose his priorities as his business grew. If you have difficulty saying 'no' to people and find yourself getting walked all over from time to time, you'll love his tips for improvement.

When The Deal's No Good, Walk Away

by Alex Petty

Business Mentor and Listener, Growth Partner, Team Motivator,
Business Owner Support and Lifesaver;
Thatcham, United Kingdom

What a lovely day to be running among the tall oak trees by the canal. The bright spring sunshine is warming my back, the grass watered by the earlier shower is wetting my feet.

Glad I put my sun hat on.

My thoughts are ranging from how I can help a client implement their financial learnings to the feeling of the stones through my trail running shoes. The large rough stones are making my feet feel sore. They are taking front of stage in my thoughts right now.

I'm rounding the bend of the canal that leads to a lock I know well. I glance at the weir and see the water sparkling as it bubbles over the vegetation-covered concrete sluice. My heavy footsteps and hard breathing startle some resting ducks, sending them scuttling and quacking into the water. They shake their tail feathers with indignation. I smile at their display of annoyance.

Not long till I can turn back towards home; I'm almost at the halfway point of my run.

My reverie is disturbed as my phone rings. Damn, I had meant to put it on silent. Still, I see the name of a previous client come up on the screen. Better answer it, I think. I've worked with this company before.

I slow to a walk and work hard to catch my breath as I answer.

"Hello, how are you, Alex?" My caller says in his buoyant, slightly superior way. I answer that I'm well and just out on a run. He ignores my comment and gets straight to business.

"We want you to work for us again!"

I never worked for you in the first place, I think to myself. Still, let's hear what he has to say. Might be profitable.

I'm instructed to turn my video on so that we can see each other. I see he's sitting back in his chair. I'm already feeling a tension rising in me.

"Okay, so what is it I can help you with?"

My previous client proceeds to offer me three options of how I can work for him. He lists his terms, and how I'll fit in to his organisation. What is expected of me and how I am to perform. How I am to behave, what I can say, and what I can't.

After talking at me for almost twenty minutes, he asks which option I choose.

I have a choice? Oh, how nice.

The look on his face when I decline. He couldn't quite work that one out. That wasn't in his plan.

He starts to explain the options again, as though, like a simpleton, I hadn't understood him the first time.

My answer is the same.

I then tell him how I would work with him - rather than for him - and my terms. He was shocked. We finished the call with vague pleasantries and hung up.

I don't think he had expected my response, but no one speaks to me like that. I learnt years ago to say 'no' to opportunities that were not favourable to me, both in terms of profit and how I'm treated.

I still get a little emotional when I feel the need to do this, and I usually overanalyse if I've made the right decision. I feel anger at the cheek of some people. I feel worried that my gut reaction is too quick to close down an opportunity. But, looking back over the years, the times I went wrong were when I didn't follow my intuition and signed up to deals which I somehow knew were not good for me.

My natural approach is to look to help people make their business better. I believe that I'm able to help anyone improve when they are ready to make changes to develop their business or personal life. I have learnt that there are people who can't, or don't, want to be helped. These are the people whom I now give a wide berth.

To help me with my decision making, I introduced a set of rules and criteria of how I will work with businesses. I remain flexible as to how I work alongside my clients, but there are some fundamental rules from which I will not deviate.

I developed these learnings from my time in corporate and from my initial foray into business. If I want my team to stick with me and respect me, they need to know that they have my support and trust. It is a two-way street.

So how did I get to the stage where I felt confident enough to turn away business that is not right for me?

It is easy to say that you won't take on work from a customer that you feel doesn't make a good fit. When it comes down to it, though, and you're under financial pressure in your business, it is all too easy to make a bad 'intuitive' decision.

I am an emotional person, driven by how I feel about something. So, here's what I did.

I removed the emotional component from the equation.

There are no hard and fast rules of how to make sure you are making the right decisions. I developed a process, nice and simple. Here are a couple of examples from my approach:

1) I make sure I know my numbers. This way I can understand from a financial perspective if this is a profitable opportunity.

I keep tabs on the amount of income I need to make to cover my running costs, pay salaries and make a profit for the business. I also know what my sales funnel looks like – impending deals about to go live.

2) I have defined the relationship rules under which I will operate. How will I interact with my team and clients and how will they be expected to behave back to me and my team? These are my operating values.

I have developed these company values for how everyone will treat each other in my business and how the customers will be treated. By default, I will always give support for my team members in the face of a difficult/unreasonable customer.

Another key factor in being able to make my decision is confidence: my confidence in myself and in my business.

From an early age, I learnt to be independent; this led to a confidence in myself and my abilities.

I developed my business confidence over time in corporate and from running my own companies. I have a good understanding of what I am capable of, what my business is capable of and how I want it to operate. I am clear on how things work. I have invested a significant amount of time developing my operating processes and offerings; this has made it easier for me to make a choice of the type of work I am looking for and the type of customer with whom I will work.

It is my choice with whom I work. I am ready to turn away from a potential opportunity if it's not the right fit for me.

I remember a lot of times when, at the start, I was not clear enough with my marketing. It placed me in front of a whole range of prospects. Unfortunately, a significant percentage were not the right fit for me or my business offering. I still remember the time I spent all day trying to sign someone up as a coaching client, only for them to say a brusque "No, thanks" at the end of it all.

With a clear lead generation and sales process, along with more focused marketing, I improved my conversion rate for the right clients.

I also learnt what it takes to operate an effective company. There are many aspects to running a business, but key is that I must know my numbers … I didn't do that right at the beginning. Now, it's a key activity in my weekly management and monitoring activities.

I defined a simple way to more objectively decide with whom I want to work.

I found it all too easy to take on work that didn't fit my core offering when things were tight financially. I learnt that it's better to bring in the right expert to cover activities outside my core skillset. Better to give the client the best service with the right team.

Within the first couple of years of my starting my company, there were times that I took on projects that I wouldn't have, had I been better off. They usually did not go as well for me as they should. What's more, I wouldn't lower my prices to win that job anymore. I found that it made for problems later on when I realised that I wasn't making enough profit, if any.

I have experienced the pain and embarrassment of working for around £1.95 per hour I put into a client. You can easily say that I'm dumb to have allowed that. Before you jump on that, though, take a look at your own hourly income. I find that many business owners are shocked when they learn how little they are getting for all their hard work.

From bitter experience, I also learnt that taking on work just to have some cash made me feel undervalued. Oh, how I resented that. It was my fault though. I allowed myself to accept that I was worth less than I should have been charging. I can be flexible with charging in certain circumstances. It is from a position of fully understanding what I will be providing for the fees and what I have removed from the offer to fit a client's budget. This way, it is an equitable relationship, good for both parties.

So, how did I get so confident? I've learnt that I'm confident with things I've worked on learning. Either from courses, tutorials and general experience of just 'giving it a go'. Typically, I am confident that I can learn what I need to. I am also confident enough to recognise when I need a subject matter expert to share the work. Better to win 50% of a good opportunity than settle for 100% of nothing.

The way I built my business confidence was by:

- Attending seminars, workshops and tutorials.

- Reading many business books – I have a large list. Soft skills, too.

- Recording my successes and mistakes so that I could learn from both. Being prepared to just do things – give them a go and learn from the results.

- Calling upon my experience from working in corporate.

- Working alongside other, more experienced business mentors and coaches to learn on the job.

- Knowing I was 'good enough'.

I remember a painful learning from my early days as a business coach. I didn't really understand business financials' when I first started coaching.

I am sitting with a client and he asks me about his financials. I stare intently at the numbers that came from his accountant. Truth is, I don't really know what it's showing me. Yes, I can see that there is less coming in than is being spent on running the business, but (how I hate that word!) I realise that I'm not in a position to offer much help.

I'll never forget how embarrassed I am.

I have to change this weakness into a strength. I'm always up for that – it's one of my strengths. I'm able to see what I need, and take the action required to get the job done.

I am honest with the client, and we resolve to get a financial expert in to help provide the guidance he needs.

That very evening, I booked myself some training. I attended financial training workshops and taught myself basic bookkeeping from the mass of online tutorials available online.

I still do my own books so that I remember what it takes. I read some great books on the topic. Very soon, I started teaching what I'd learnt – the best way to get good at something is to teach it. I had to get it right.

Through a lot of study and practical experience, I have gained a good understanding of financials for running a business. Of course, I will still always recommend an accountant, a bookkeeper, an IFA for those areas outside my remit.

Now, as I slow my pace to a walk, I look to the trees at the side of canal for inspiration. They offer a calming effect as they gently wave to me. I'm reminded to use my checklist to help me decide if I want to take the opportunities offered:

- Like/don't like

- Trust/don't trust

- Respect/don't respect

- Financially stable/need the cash now

- The opportunity fits what I do/does not fit what I do.

Like/Don't Like

It is all too easy to turn away a good opportunity when I don't feel that I like someone. As a coach, the client and I need to like and respect each other. But it doesn't mean I have to fully agree with their view of the world. In fact, some of my greatest learnings have come from seeing other people's point of view.

Conversely, liking someone too much can make for a difficult working relationship. I always advocate a stronger set of rules when working with a friend. That way, the work gets done and the friendship remains intact. I would go so far as to say that if you can't separate the two relationships objectively, then don't work together.

Trust/Don't Trust

Trust is everything. It is a core part of my maintaining my integrity. I work from the premise that I believe that people are basically good.

Whilst I've had a few times when people have let me down, it is a specific positive occasion that I'm recalling in which I learned that trust is everything.

I believe that the only thing I really own is my integrity. I will not compromise on that. Trust is the same. If there is a shadow of doubt, then there is no trust. If I feel that I cannot trust someone, I find it very difficult to work with them.

Respect/Don't Respect

It is more important to me that I am respected rather than liked. Respect can be a feeling of deep admiration for someone or something elicited by their abilities, qualities, and/or achievements. Also, giving due regard for the feelings, wishes, or rights of someone else. One of the greatest confidence boosters for me was when someone I held in high regard let me know of their respect for my achievements.

Financially Stable/Need The Cash Now

I have experienced times when things were financially tight for me. I found that I was running to every prospective opportunity to earn some funds.

This had a number of negative effects. When I took on work just for the money, it was often at the expense of my own self-worth and at a risk to not being the best person for a client. There have been times that I begrudged the work and lower income, or the client didn't get a level of service that they should have.

I decided that I would not take on work 'at any cost'. Sometimes, it's about more than the money. Even at the standard charge rate, it wouldn't be enough to make the deal a good one for me.

I experienced how it was all too easy to reduce my prices just to get some cash coming in. I even told myself that I'd put the prices up later, or that I'd get better clients soon …

It didn't happen like that. I have never found a customer who wants to pay more than the price I started charging them for my services.

It seems that everyone expects a discount these days. The way I deal with price challenges is to say, "Yes, I can reduce the price. What would you like me to leave out?"

The Opportunity Fits What I Do/Does Not Fit What I Do

I choose to work with clients within the remit of what my company offers. I stick to what I do well; I stick to what I enjoy doing and in a way that suits me and my business. That doesn't rule out some flexibility, although I make sure the scope of the job doesn't go outside what I am here to do. As before, I get an expert in when they are required; they will do a much better job than I, and that means a happy client.

To make sure I work with the right people, on the right projects and programmes, I have a list of what I offer and what is included. I make this clear during a complimentary coaching call or session. I make sure that my marketing clearly reflects what I offer.

As I respectfully educate my caller, I feel balanced, centred and in control. Having carefully explained how any forward working together will go, we politely finish the call.

I look out across the canal and notice the long feathery reed heads on the opposite bank, dancing skittishly in the strengthening breeze. The wind playfully making ripples on the dark waters.

Time to turn around and run back home. After a couple of minutes, I feel my breathing settling back in rhythm with my legs.

What approach do you take to decide if you are going to work with someone or not?

To find out more: alex@alexpetty.biz
                      www.alexpetty.biz

KEY 3: SUPPORT

Have you ever leaned on your family or friends for support with your business? Many business owners do. In fact, the Bank of America conducted a survey in 2016 (their 'Small Business Owner Report') and found that half of the one thousand respondents depended on those close to them personally to perform crucial roles in their business.

It's not always financial support that business owners seek, as you might think. Very often, they're driven by a need for operational help and even emotional and social support.

Why not? We are supposed to enjoy each other's company, after all. Have a solid network around you in the workplace can ultimately be the 'make or break' of your business. If you cannot enjoy what you do, or share it in any way, you'll eventually run out of passion for it. It helps to have a sense of balance between work and play on a daily level, and that's one of the most important things that other people can bring to your business life.

Nearly sixty per cent of those interviewed in the survey reported their having depended on close friends or family members for emotional support since they started their business. Not all of the anxieties and difficulties that go hand in hand with starting up and running a business can be put right with money. A lot of them performed volunteer roles in the business or became involved in skill sharing or running machinery without pay.

If the idea of asking for financial support from someone close to you makes your blood run cold, it may make you feel a bit better to know that thirteen per cent of the business owners asked said that their spouse or family paid for their groceries, clothing and household costs in the early days. Few people who asked for financial help felt awkward doing so, possibly because they fully intended to reimburse the giver.

How nice to know that you have people on side, though! Irrespective of what you need their support for, just having a good team around you can lift your spirits and turn your grey skies to blue. A positive mindset will always be better for your business than a negative one.

Do you have good people around you? Is there a space where someone you love or simply respect would fit in perfectly?

When Indu found herself with an 'empty nest' when her daughter left home for university, she faced a whole new set of circumstances in her personal life. It coincided with a time of growth and change for her business as well as for her, and she found the support of those whom she trusted crucial to see her through. The next is her story …

Winds of Change

by Indu Varanasi

Design Director at IRD Design. Inspired in design, disciplined in action
United Arab Emirates

Change happens. Perhaps this is the only constant, as they say.

Change is viewed in different ways for different things, at different times. My story starts at a point where most people would say, "Do we really want continue this or take it a bit easy after all these years?"

But life is cyclical, like the seasons: you see rain, hope for the sunshine, you see the sunshine and wait for the cooler seasons and for the sun to peep through the clouds in winter … so the story goes on. We see this year after year, never tiring.

It is a thought which passes my mind, each time I see my daughter as she grows up. I often wonder about all the seasons we go through.

Often, I see myself in her and muse on the next of steps of the journey. So many moments of sun, rain and hail we cherish as parents. The first birthday, the first day of school, each parent teacher meeting, sports days, the umpteen plays, the art classes, the continuous chatter of friends. The flurry of activity before high school finishes, the anxiety of university admissions and then suddenly it is time to leave home to go to university.

What follows is a strange silence.

I always wonder what my parents thought when I left for university, especially my mother who would attend my every need and even be awake at night during my exams. She never expressed herself and kept the silence she was engulfed in.

The silence around me, the vacuum and then the sudden change in pace of life was something I had anticipated but like all things, when reality hits, one is never ready for it.

While I pined for the call of, 'Mom! I can't find this or that," or, "Mom! I need to go now!" or, 'Mom! I forgot my exam ..," and so on, the silence was like meditation. A new sense of freedom, an empty mind opened up. It was like opening a door onto an horizon of endless sea.

I suddenly wondered and said to myself:

"I want to find myself in me."

After all, before being a wife and a mother, I was also a professional architect. A profession I cherished from my childhood, studied for eight years and practiced for twenty-five. It was time to change focus.

So, I looked at my other 'baby': my business and my profession. Having nurtured it carefully through the years, it was time to pay full attention to it.

This second baby was seventeen years old and at a threshold of the next journey in its life cycle.

This was my company, "I R DESIGN".

It was birthed in 2004 and I nurtured it through the years of growth from infancy to now; it was like a human being slowly changing form. Like my daughter, the company was on the verge of something new.

Most designers and architects want to work on their own; they cherish the freedom to think of themselves as the 'creator', the solution provider and making people happy in the places in which they live, work and play.

My having a design studio was a dream, a virtual entity.

Starting one in a foreign country had its own challenges. Bringing it to reality, opening it and naming it IRD was like slowly walking along an unknown path.

The path was trodden with success, failures, ups and downs and I threw a lot of tantrums on the way.

Its seventeenth year was the teenage phase of self-doubt. Like those years, when high school finishes and you are asked to choose your profession, it was a time of reckoning.

The indecision, the unknown direction of growth and collaboration, the choice of projects and choice of clients … all of these need to come together to develop a direction, a path, a plan to go forward.

Life-changing decisions are often taken in the late teens. At the threshold of going to university, the decision of what career to take becomes a crucial one. The life of a doctor is quite different from that of an engineer or a restaurateur, but it still takes a crucial decision.

It is at this time when a personality evolves from being a totally dependent child to an independent voice.

It was at this stage in 2019 that IRD needed to take an independent decision - to leverage what was built, to take the next leap.

And to create what could be lasting legacy.

The Search: What Next?

As a strategic decision of my own journey as a person with multiple identities, the Professional, the Mother, among others, I wanted to take this journey to the next level of professional development and lead towards the good of society and humanity at large.

There is big chance that when a void hits, you start wondering what will fill it. On a personal level, the home became a 'void'. Work was an extension of myself and helped to fill this big, gaping hole which I would have fallen into.

If I hadn't taken this decision as my priority, I might have been looking into another version of myself. I have seen this happen to many of my friends: they give up everything for their children, spouse and extended family and when the identity of their being is lost, they are lost.

I did not want to be there.

It was time to make the sacrifices necessary to build the company; to juggle home and office with the various associated activities linked to it.

Time to take the next leap.

Come Sept 2019, I started preparing to get into the next gear.

The first thing I noticed was that I needed to speak to people about the company as a businesswoman, even to the closest of my friends. I had always avoided this topic with them, despite the accolades and awards over the years. There was something I was missing: these people could be my biggest support structure.

Introspection was the key. The first person I spoke to was Anna, my Italian sister (because we think so much alike) and my partner. Anna is brutally frank, never sugar coats her words.

"I know how good you are but does the world know? Think about all those people who don't know anything about you," she challenged. "When I refer you to my friends, they can't find you. You know, Indu, this is the Digital Age. You need to be found up there in the virtual world too. And you'd better start thinking about this fast!"

As usual, Anna had the hit nail on the head and very hard.

I thought about it carefully. The words "people don't know you" rang in my head. What was it that I should do differently in this noisy world, with everyone claiming to be the best with the most different solutions? Design and architecture were heading in a sad direction with Instagram images becoming its showcase - almost treating design as a 'beauty without brains'.

This was the test I needed to take a stand and create awareness.

Who would understand the depth of this thought process and be able to translate it into the best marketing, positioning the company with a message to the outside world? The message to those who don't know anything about us?

The search for multiple channels and different thoughts began to happen. I began to feel excited about the new 'place' I was about explore for myself and my company. What should we do? Grow 'big' in size? Expand to different geographies? Start collaborations? Mergers?

However, growth strategy for someone who so far had just grown organically and without a plan was so difficult. I found it hard to put everything on to paper, convey the thought in a succinct and yet powerful manner because there is an overdose of information.

We all plan different things in life. Life itself takes over, though, and some plans we forget, some we have to forget and some we choose to forget. Then, there are those we remember and somehow make happen. Do we plan all this? Perhaps yes and no.

At the threshold of all this exciting possibility, I began inviting people into the office for a conversation to see how we could align ourselves, how they were thinking of growing their own field.

In all these years, I have noticed that all businesses are pretty much the same. Eighty per cent of them struggle with the same issues: staffing, payments, getting new clients and so on. The other twenty per cent involves specialising into specific fields of expertise.

At this stage, there were many options for the company. We could stay where we were, in a very niche market, with the status quo or to find collaborations and leave a legacy.

The second option required a lot of work towards the path unknown and sometimes untrodden - but this was the path I wanted to take. I needed a sounding board: someone with whom I could speak freely without feeling judged. Anna was always there but I needed someone here, in Dubai, who understood the nuances.

This option was the more difficult perhaps, more challenging in more ways than one, but this was it. I had already created a company which had challenged the process of design; I wanted to shout louder and clearer, make the change that needed to happen, but how?

Experimentation With The Unknown

As I was toying with the idea of how to work the growth at the end of 2019, there was something of a boom in the construction market. Everyone wanted to change or build something new. The market was flush with new ideas, funds, investors and all the mechanisms which make for a thriving economy.

Following suit, IRD was flooded with projects. Our focus shifted from building the company towards legacy to delivering the projects. By January 2020, IRD had more than ten projects in hand, three on-going, four signed off and three about to be signed off.

The notion was how to deliver the projects, where to get the right staff to fuel this spurt in project growth. It was all about planning it well.

Ex-colleagues from India were mobilized. Mubashir had been on the IRD team long enough to understand the ethos of the company. We had a long conversation on how I wanted to build a new out-source team in India, in Hyderabad, my hometown and how he should start looking for suitable people. We decided that the design concepts would be done in Dubai under my watchful eye.

Our choosing the right team for both here and there was important. Part of the team who worked from Dubai knew that Mubashir was not an easy person to work with. I liked his meticulousness to detail, though, his watchful eye to see if we had missed out anything. This was a dual role of developing and documenting ideas from the city of Dubai, the city of dreams.

I was happy that things were shaping up.

We were trying to leverage technology to keep the connection. We expanded our software reach so that everyone in Dubai and Hyderabad could access the same files through a dedicated server in the office.

At this time, I started talking to some of my close friends. Meenu was somebody who loved to meet people. She knew people whom she could also leverage, and our friendship grew into a business relationship.

We spent some time speaking about what to look for in potential connections within her circle. I really wanted to grow and to develop Meenu to be a self-sufficient business development support for IRD. While I was training her slowly, I also knew that it would require a far greater effort and I was ready to make it.

Then, March 2020 and everything began to change. With the lockdown, life froze. All was at a stand-still.

The unknown hit hard.

I sat at home and thought of how to manage these projects with staff working from home. A system needed to be figured out.

Some lived in shared accommodation, where everyone worked in a shared space. Some struggled with an unstable internet feed, others had small children who needed constant care. The home atmosphere was not conducive for some of my colleagues. We all made an effort and tried to create a schedule of morning and evening 'link up' sessions, which took longer than expected. Many a time, it was so difficult to communicate a simple idea in words; after all, we are the people who draw better than we talk.

Somehow, we all kept our spirits up and worked through the six weeks of complete lockdown and gradually returned to the office, working partially.

So much changed in the meantime, though. Within the span of six weeks, the market sentiment altered completely: nobody wanted to build anymore and a sense of fear was all pervasive. Every single new project was put on hold. The company's growth stalled.

Nothing moved, all was at a standstill.

And so was I.

We breathe, life goes on till our last breath. We need to keep moving.

After the initial fear subsided, I had to make myself think differently, do things I had never done before, act as if I was starting all over again. What would I do differently or what should I have known?

There was something which struck me: 'the business of design'.

I had thrived professionally. The design practice helped to explore different aspects of design which I had never done before. I had learnt how carpenters work their skill while working with wood, which type of wood is used and where, what types of veneers are there and how they are cut and so many such nuances which are taken for granted in the larger design practices where there is a specialist for everything. It is the learning of new things and unlearning of many such details which led me to thrive in my own field.

The business of design was learning how to read balance sheets and Profit & Loss statements, but it was at this crucial juncture in 2020 when the world seemed to stand still that I began to think that the business needed more. I was missing some fundamentals, some aspects which needed to be looked at without any emotion.

An idea started forming in my mind …

This business was our investment of time, money and energy. This should also be our means to lead a comfortable life later. But who would take it on once I could no longer work? What would make it a 'business' rather than just a passion-driven design practice?

To add to it all, my son took up product design as a profession. The next generation did not seem interested carrying on this business or contribute to it in any way.

What needed to change? I had no idea. I guess nobody had but we could not sit and watch for the water to recede.

The dilemma was so great that my mind was spinning at a thousand miles an hour. I was going dizzy with everything around me fading. Some may have despaired, but I am a fighter and found good days here and there. I guess we are all human after all.

At this point, I chanced upon Rob Goddard's LinkedIn post. It was a very interesting topic about an having 'exit' plan. Although I had heard business leaders say that you should have an exit plan before you start a company, being a non-conformist I hated the idea of leaving something even before starting it.

Rob and I had some correspondence. We exchanged emails and something like an 'interview' on Zoom. Each of us was trying to figure out if the other was the right fit. I loved Rob's confidence and he was wondering if I was really a businesswoman or just someone so passionate about what I was doing that the 'business' part of it was completely forgotten. I could almost see him chuckle.

On the other hand, I guessed he also realised the sincerity with which I was running the business and sensed how I needed help to convey this different approach towards the design in the building industry. After all the hard work and a portfolio of some wonderful projects, nobody knew us. Therefore, we did not exist. There is no price for something which is not seen or heard. Intrinsic value is not just the marketing but also believing in marketing.

This was a shift in my thinking, kind of realization, a mental shift and a new approach. Another chapter began. It was the unknown. The journey with Rob required a year's commitment into something which was not at all my field. My having been 'coach agnostic' all through my life, I wanted to figure out everything myself.

Collaborating and Committing

The first sessions were about introducing ourselves. Oh, my - what a diverse group, profession wise, age wise and goal wise! I found it fascinating that such a motley group had come together. And to add to it, I was the only one in the beginning who was not English and missed some of the jokes and puns ... huh!

Rob was doing his best to keep everyone engaged and also making sure that the alien in the room (in other words, me), was feeling at home by sharing his own experience of Dubai with its highs and lows.

One of the first sessions was about our own challenges and what we were feeling the most 'caught-up' with.

Colin went in first with his story. In that session, I was totally lost. What did this guy do, actually? He was so figured out with business terminology, matrix, costs, analyses ... Oh, well, I did not understand most of it but loved the passion with which he spoke. I also tried to look at the website, not that I understood that any better. That's me and business, I thought.

Then it was my turn. I was nervous, so lost on how I should say what I wanted to say. I had simple words but big problems. I needed to survive and needed to say it clearly to this private group. If they could not understand me, then no one would. I resolved to give it a shot and see what they had to say.

I explained as well as I could that the design studio had broken barriers and thresholds on the design frontier bringing good design solutions where none existed. We had seized the 'white space', so to speak. As I thought thinking about all the past and how this growth was achieved, I thought I should re-visit all the projects.

It's as if you sit down and go through a 'photo album. My daughter's album, from the day she was born; the little one cuddled in your arms, to the faltering steps, the mischievous smile after rubbing chocolate all over her face or the crying at the start of the new school day. There are so many memories.

As I start recalling all such moments there are some parallels in business. Do we treat our business as a 'living' organism, something which we love and is equally breathing and eating? It needs to be fed and loved as any other living thing. It was something profound which stirred me.

Being a solo entrepreneur, the journey of nurturing this business was akin to looking after a baby. Why did I not think of it the same way?

Was it just me or could everyone think of theirs in the same way?

Is there a real emotion attached to your company, and do you actually think of it as a part of you and a part of the living eco-system around you?

The heart wrenching tug of letting go, the tug of sharing your 'baby' with the world ... knowing that, however difficult it is, it needs to be done. From moments of going to school, the dance classes, the art classes, the sports sessions, all knowing that this 'baby' is going to be scolded, perhaps hurt physically and emotionally. We go through it all and all-knowingly.

This churn of events, a subtext to the calculating world of business, is perhaps not visible to many. They don't look at it as something which is done day in and day out. So much of our time and energy is devoted our work and livelihood that, in most cases, we forget that this is Life. There is no 'work life' and 'another life': all is Life and living. How we choose to live is in our hands.

With these thoughts in the background, I narrated my story to the group. I told them of how I'd reached a threshold and of how I needed to look at the next leap. How I was totally lost on how to do it. The growth pangs started to hit.

Each of them had their own perspective and viewpoint, narrated in their distinctive styles: Michelle with her beautiful articulation of the passion of business, Colin with his insightful analysis of the problem, John looking at the numbers, Paul giving the sales suggestion and Rob articulating my issue in clear, concise terms, ending with "Do it!"

The universal consensus was 'delegate'.

It was a moment to let go. Let go of the complete control and see how others can perform the role that you normally would.

Actually, nothing much was happening. We were only fine-tuning our systems which sometimes became a bit boring, so there was not harm trying at all.

A Ray at The End of The Tunnel

The primary source of income was only through sale of Interior Design services, so complementary services should be introduced.

I started talking to people that I knew. Suddenly, there were people who really wanted to join the team. It is so strange that we don't value what we have before then. IRD in their eyes was a big entity, has made its mark. Whatever was happening now was just a blip - but I was nervous.

I invited Leema to join me to take on small residential projects within a small projects division. Anything less than US$150k would be taken up as a design and build and she would handle everything from design to delivery.

On the same note, a very old friend, one of the first I met when I came to Dubai in 1994 evolved as a project manager. Rakesh, a civil engineer by profession, joined us to provide specialised project management services.

Finally, Kishore joined, too, providing architectural services.

Rob also helped create a vision board which would give me a clear thinking of where and how I should achieve my goals, business and financial, going right back to the question, "How do I grow the business to be able to sell it?"

This was much more difficult than I imagined. I was so clear in my thinking up until then - and how wrong was I.

Our team was complete but there were still no jobs on the market and we were still stalling. As the year came to an end, the winds were changing, the market was shrugging off its nervousness. We were hearing of projects being awarded but nothing was landing on our plate.

Always late!

What was going on? How come we couldn't reach out to any of our past clients? What was happening? Another piece of the puzzle was missing. We thought and thought, but took no action ...

It was about that time that I had my chance to put a challenge to Rob's group.

In my head it was so complicated: I made Excel sheets, put down things like 'opportunity costs', 'walk-way pricing' and whatnot. I spent hours on calculating how to make everything work.

As I narrated my challenge, I grumbled, fumed and grunted that I was missing opportunities because of no particular reason.

What happened next was revealing.

Each person of the group started dissecting the problem and each one, in their own way, knew exactly what the problem was. It was as though I was the one who could not see what they were seeing. Was I blind? It seemed so.

Colin, Alex, Rob and Paul all agreed that I needed a structured business development and salesperson on board immediately.

This person should be well-versed with the market, come with some contacts, a background of the industry and should be able to convey the ethos of the company besides the 'sale' being the motivating factor.

The search began. I told friends, industry colleagues and recruitment agencies. I sat through many interviews. All the candidates had sold tangible products, anything from furniture to flooring to lights to fabric, everything one could touch and feel - but I needed someone who could sell ideas.

Ideas are all in the head. Nobody can touch them or feel them. One can only react to them, imagine them and fly to another world. How could I find an aggressive salesperson who is sensitive to nuance, too?

While all this was brewing, the funds in the office were depleting at a very fast rate. How quickly so much money becomes so little when there is no source to replenish it. The drip, drip, drip was emptying the tank, as it were.

The only way forward was to take the risk and get someone on board as soon as possible. Fortunately, my prayers were answered when a neighbour who had seen an article on me in some industry magazine, walked up to me and said she was in the same industry. As we spoke, she revealed that she was the Marketing Manager of a well-known contractor. I asked her if she knew of anyone who was looking out for a job in Business Development.

In three days, she came back to me. She said that her ex-colleague was looking for an opportunity and would like to meet. He was looking to represent a good company.

This guy was Akash – a young man, a few years older than my son, brash, arrogant but highly intelligent. Although not the refined, sophisticated person I would have liked, I considered him an uncut diamond. I was willing to take the chance. My emotions were so strong that I wanted to take advice from others.

Kishore and Rakesh took another interview. Both said a big NO. Too arrogant, they said.

The final interview was with Rob.

His feedback was, "He has the hunger. Hire him and see."

Akash was hired six weeks ago, and yesterday we gave our first presentation.

I hope this is the path to recovery.

It's been a tough path. I've bordered on despair, and we've all fought. There are many things which happen unknowingly.

To be philosophical, I know there is purpose to my life.

I will fulfil it. There are people sent to guide us, help and take us along this journey knowingly or unknowingly.

To find out more: indu@irdesign.co
www.irdesign.co

KEY 4: THREAT

If you've been in business for any length of time, you'll already know how much of a rollercoaster ride it is. Clients and colleagues will come and go, you'll have good and bad months and your vision will change as often as you take a weekend off.

The biggest threat isn't to your business, though: it's to you. Your business will respond to whatever action you take to further it or sabotage it ... the choice is yours. Your actions follow your thoughts, and your thoughts respond to your emotions. So, how are you doing, emotionally?

Are you able to withstand the threats that face every entrepreneur at some stage?

Here are the top five most common threats to personal wellbeing that business owners say they face, often more than once:

- Burnout

- Depression

- Financial worries

- Overwork

- Failing relationships

When we suffer from any or a mix of these, our businesses suffer, too. Your business is there to support you – if not immediately, then eventually. The one thing that we all strive for is that elusive 'happiness', whatever form that takes.

Are you clued up enough to recognise the signs of any of these threats were they to crop up in your life? Do you know what to do, who to turn to if they do?

If you've entered the business owning lifestyle without counting the cost completely, don't worry. Few of us do. Most young businesses 'fail' because their owners thought that growing it would be a breeze ... until it turned into a gale.

You don't need to work around the clock to make a success of your business. You do need to research how business life can affect you, though, and how others get through the storms you will face.

These things affect your psyche, your emotional wellbeing, and ultimately your physical health, too. If you don't put yourself first, your business can't hope to support you. And that's what it's there for, after all.

- There are things that you can do right now to safeguard yourself against the threats to your wellbeing that entrepreneurship can pose:

- Create a realistic business plan that excites you

- Get someone else whom you trust and who understands entrepreneurship to look at your business plan and ask them for feedback

- Keep your friends and family out of your business life (unless you're running a family business, of course)

- Keep your friends and family at the centre of your personal life

- Prioritise who's truly important in your life and treasure them

- Don't wait for someone else to come up with solutions for you. Believe in yourself, lean on your support group and make your own decisions

Remember, you're not the only one who's felt small, displaced and abandoned from time to time. Everyone who's started a business has faced threats to their psychological wellbeing at some point. Talk to others, allow them to help you grow your stamina and decision-making skills.

In this next story, Joanna found out that her vulnerability to chaotic circumstances and personal loss was the biggest threat to her business. She tuned in to her instincts and emotions, stopped waiting for things to come right on their own and made some tough decisions. She took action and made the right changes – for herself and for her business.

Moving On

by Joanna Collie

Author, Ghostwriter and Writing Mentor. Putting the ZING into your writing. Owner and Founder of the Authorship Mentor Programme (AMP) Salisbury, United Kingdom

"Durn't you stend there making arse at me, lady!"

The passport control officer was scaling dizzy heights of rage very quickly.

I faced a dilemma: I could a) stand up to the ex-Eighties cop and make a gesture for feminism that nobody would remember, or b) allow my eyes to dip, offer a demure curtsey and hope that I could still get out of here before I was arrested.

The problem was, I was wearing the obligatory mask. All that showed on my face were my eyes and eyebrows – and my left eyebrow was rogue.

Ever since I was a kid, my left eyebrow had heaped trouble onto me. It has a life of its own: arching up in a shot the moment my brain triggers anything odd, stupid, questionable, ironic, funny or just plain wrong. It annoys some, makes others laugh.

This one was annoyed.

"I know your tarp!" he spat. "You Bruts just thunk you ken do what you lark…"

Twang – my left eyebrow shot up in a dramatic arch, pulling half of my face with it with an extra-effort hoik towards my hairline.

He might have been one of those cops I could remember from 1984 in Cape Town, when I was a gormless, English teenager freshly arrived during the State of Emergency towards the end years of apartheid.

Look, it'll take forever to explain. It boils down to my having dual citizenship: I belong both to the UK and to South Africa. I had travelled to Cape Town on my British passport, and because my flight home had been cancelled, the travel visa in it had expired four months ago. Not that I had needed it, though, as I hold South African citizenship, too.

This chap didn't like that, though. I dipped my eyes and tried a quick curtsey.

You don't mess about in South Africa. Especially when there's a pandemic on and only one flight available back to the UK.

When you have a dysfunctional family, your friends take their place in your life. My friends are my family, really, and when my best friend of thirty-six years started ghosting me after her mother died, there was nothing more important for me to do than to hop on an aeroplane and fly to her in Cape Town. She had stopped communicating with me, telling me that she was a shadow of her former self and I lived too far away in the UK.

We had been joined at the hip for years. We were godmother to each other's children. When our mutual friends thought of one of us, they'd think of the other, too. This couldn't happen to us. We were 'bezzers' for life, weren't we?

I needed to see her face to face, find out what was really going on and help her. I could go for five months – I could run my business from wherever I liked, really – and that should be long enough to sort it out.

We would be back to normal soon.

Five months back in Cape Town was an exciting prospect. I'd get to see all of my old friends, visit my favourite spots and miss the UK winter. I might even get to perform again with some of my old musician pals.

I put my things in storage and moved out of my place in Ealing, wondering where I'd end up when I came back to the UK. Although London was good for networking, I missed the countryside. I needed to build the business over the next five months and then I'd be free to head back to the South West, where I grew up.

As an author, ghostwriter and writing mentor, I'd been focusing on taking on a couple of clients at a time for several months. It wasn't the best plan; I could see that I was putting all of my eggs in one basket much of the time, which made me nervous. I should produce my mentoring and training as tutorials and courses as soon as I could find the time. That way, I could take on more clients at a lower cost, selling my courses and books online as a residual income.

As soon as I could find the time, of course. Right now, I had two books to finish and was working on a pitch for a new client, which would be a big one.

My first port of call was my old friend, Miree. We'd met when we started working at a brand new, talk radio station in Cape Town back in 1997. I was Head of Creative and she was Marketing Manager, roles that we kept over the years in other companies as we moved on from Cape Talk. I had moved back to the UK and stayed in radio, writing advertising campaigns, promos and competitions and training writers until my last role was made redundant. Now, I was flying solo, while Miree worked with an entertainment company.

I couldn't wait to catch up with her over a bottle of wine in her leafy garden, laugh about the early days and get her opinion on what on earth was going on with Shelley. We'd been looking forward to our reunion for weeks.

I took a couple of days after landing to sort myself out with accommodation and then belted round to her cottage.

When she answered my rap on her door, my lovely friend's eyes were preoccupied and frightened.

"I found a lump in my breast, Josie," she spoke in a low, whispery voice. "They operated a couple of days ago and I start chemo next week."

I found a little studio close to Miree's place – a cottage in someone's garden, really – which was light, airy and kitted out with all the bits I needed. I could use it as my base for five months and afford to move around the country to visit friends.

The first three months of my stay passed in a hot blur. There was no aircon in my little studio, so I spent the whole of summer working in a sarong next to a rickety old fan on full blast.

I didn't mind; I had my patio area, a pretty garden with the familiar view of the mountain. It made a pleasant change to my huddling next to a heater at this time of the year ... although my eyes went through their own, peculiar hell.

In a year that the pollen count in Cape Town was at its highest on record, I was allergic to every tree in my garden as well as the flora all over the mountainside.

I streamed itchy, salty tears for weeks. Nothing that the GP prescribed would stop it. I would simply have to wait until March, when the season would finish having its wicked way with me. I met my old friends with a splodgy, swollen face – ruining my own entrance at every party after my absence of eight years.

The security was a riddle, too. The burglar alarm was chiefly controlled from the main house. I could arm my windows and doors, but if my landlady or landlord inadvertently armed my studio from their side when they went out, I couldn't move without blasting the entire valley with ear-splitting horror.

Every time the alarm went off, the security chaps would come winding their way through the garden towards my cottage, ready to annihilate anyone who wasn't supposed to be there.

At first, it freaked me out. Then, I felt ashamed and apologetic. Finally, I despaired and stretched a sock over the beam on my patio door, rendering it useless and me helpless in case of an attack. I figured I'd take my chances, although I couldn't get rid of the knot of sickly fear in my stomach from then on as I sat outside in the evenings.

I remembered how I had used to feel as a single mother living just around the corner. The fear of crime and the stress that went with it was there constantly and we had all learned to live with it twenty years ago. Mine had mostly dissipated since my move to the UK; I'd forgotten what it was like.

As lovely as Cape Town was, I wouldn't want to live with that again. I felt a wave of sympathy for my friends. Perhaps that was one of the things that had affected Shelley so deeply. Who wouldn't be affected by that?

The second book was prepped, proofed and ready to go. My old laptop had done me proud, hanging on to what life it had left with grim determination and a grinding fan. I'd need to replace it soon, especially as the battery seemed to losing power more quickly. I pushed my chair away from the kitchen table and stood up, stretching with relief.

The alarm went off for the seventh time that day, sock or no. My landlord had gone away for the weekend, leaving towel flapping on the back of a poolside chair on his side of the property. Each time, within a few minutes, the predictable torch beams approached through the back garden as the security watch obligingly came to my rescue.

"Okay, Madam – no worries. We're here to help. I'll let the owner know."

Surely, now, with the sock in place and the towel confiscated, I would be left in peace.

Overall, though, it had been a good day.

Earlier, I'd had a three-way call to the CEO and chairman of the company with which I'd been negotiating, and the contract was worked out. I would work on a part-time employment basis for them for three days a week developing and producing a series of books under their own publishing name. I'd be paid £3k per month and still have time to run my own ghostwriting business.

I felt the stress lift from my shoulders … I'd done it! I wouldn't face the kind of money worries I'd had since losing my job again.

The alarm could go off as much as it liked. I was on Cloud Nine.

Heading home from a party in Hout Bay with old friends the following Saturday, I watched the world go by from the back of the car and admired the scene. The brilliant blue of the ocean seemed to reflect in the air, dazzling and dancing light that is unique to Cape Town. It truly is one of the world's most beautiful places. And now that Uber was a thing, it was a lot easier to get about and enjoy a couple of drinks without having to drive.

How sophisticated, I thought, as I happily let the driver take control.

"You smell very delicious …" he purred.

I froze in the backseat. What did he just say?

"Your scent reminds me of a wet forest on a spring day," he murmured, completely oblivious to the look of shock that must have been plastered all over my face had he looked in his rearview mirror.

Normally, I'd be delighted to discover an Uber driver who was an aspiring novelist. Now, though, I was locked alone in a speeding vehicle on a freeway in one of the world's most dangerous places.

If I made it back to the studio, I'd hire a car immediately for the remaining two months of my stay.

Stumbling through the door, I beelined for my laptop, slapping on the light switch as I threw my bag on the table.

Nothing happened.

I looked at the light switch, then the bulb. Must have blown. Strangely, though, the laptop was dead, too. Were we having a power failure?

My phone had a little life left in it.

"Miree, do you have power? My electricity is off."

"No, honey – we're all out. It's loadshedding," she couldn't hide the surprised note in her voice. "Didn't you know? It's something we've all had to get used to around here."

She tried to explain something about the national grid's being overdue for repairs and how it affected the infrastructure of the whole country's power; how the government had come up with the patchy solution of switching it off regionally on a daily basis for anything between two and eight hours at a time.

The last time it had happened was about a year earlier, but now they needed to do it again.

"How long is this going to carry on? How does anyone run a business?" I couldn't believe my ears.

"Who knows?" she groaned. "Might be for months. Maybe for good. You normally have a few hours' notice in the Western Cape, so it gives you time to fire up your computer battery and stock up on candles. It can be quite cosy, but your alarm won't work, so best stay inside."

Bloody hell.

Over the next few days, I stocked up with candles for the hours I'd be without electricity. My laptop battery would only last an hour and it was getting weaker all the time, so I had to think carefully about how to manage my work hours. I could structure books, chapters and content articles with a good old-fashioned pen and paper but writing and research would have to take a backseat when the lights were out.

Well, I thought. That must be it, now. There can't possibly be any further nasty surprises.

Lockdown hit South Africa three days after it started in the UK. I had just been for my first drive in my little hire car down to the beach and heard the news on the radio on the way back.

Nobody was allowed to leave home – even to exercise. Shopping was to be done at your most local store, and anyone caught driving further than that would be arrested. The beaches were closed as of now. Alcohol and cigarettes were banned outright.

President Cyril Ramaphosa addressed the nation in a grave voice. "You will do lockdown sober."

I had a quarter of a bottle of white wine in my fridge. I poured it into a glass and looked at it mournfully. This would be the last sip I'd have for months. If ever I really fancied a full bottle, it was now.

Three weeks into my new contract and just a fortnight into lockdown, my employers in the UK were panicking. People began to get laid off and furloughed.

I could see the writing on the wall: my number was just about up as I was still on probation. Last one in, first one out. When the confirmation came that the contract couldn't go ahead, I felt doomed.

I had turned work down to take on the contract. It comprised three quarters of my income ... what was I supposed to do now? Like so many others around the world, I was staring into the hairy face of the wolf at the door again.

By now, it wasn't just my best friend who felt so near and yet so far. It was the whole world. I was stuck in my one-roomed studio alone for the next eight weeks.

My landlord took to running around the perimeter of the property, including my garden, which helped me to remember what human beings look like. I joined in with him soon, as I realised I'd run out of food early and end up twice my normal size if I didn't get some exercise.

I wasn't completely bereft of company, though. I had the birds and the squirrels, all of whom I named and chatted to in the mornings and early evenings when they popped by.

"This is it," I thought. "I'm actually losing my mind."

I felt threatened by virtually everything: my painful friendship that seemed to be over, the cancer that was threatening Miree, daily blackouts that cut off the alarm and left me vulnerable and lonely, toxic trees in the only outside space I could use and the insurmountable obstacle of having to find enough new business to replace my lost contract.

To top it all off, I had a car that I couldn't use sitting in my driveway, all paid for with no refund.

I had another couple of months of this to get through. Sober.

The lockdown silence reverberated against the mountainside. The Southern Suburbs of Cape Town transformed into a massive amphitheatre.

It gave me a sense of how things used to be: every small thing was amped to its max – the songbird, the cricket, the starling, the squirrel .

Pap, pap, pap! Pap, pap, pap!

What the hell was that? It racketed around the quiet neighbourhood like a terrorist attack. My landlord was shooting squirrels on his side of the property. My squirrels. My friends!

Was nothing sacred?

Speaking of friends, things with Shelley weren't improving, either. I thought that the pandemic might have changed her mind a bit and I texted her.

"I'm still here, Bez – why don't we have a call? How are you guys doing stuck at home?"

The response was a stomach cruncher.

"I hope you have a lovely time, but I want things to stay the same."

Was this for real? I wanted to rush over, demand to know from this imposter what she'd done with my friend. She had already said several times that I had done nothing wrong, but I continued to search for anything that I might have said or done that might have triggered this.

I read up on other people's experience of their having been 'ghosted' by a close friend, how the ghostee often feels guilty without knowing why and traumatised from the lack of 'closure'. They all said what I was feeling: losing that special person was like losing a part of yourself.

"This is such bad luck, Josie," my Cape Town friends cooed on a group WhatsApp call one evening. "We've hardly seen you yet, and it's been years since you were last here. You're hardly having a fun stay, are you?"

I loved them for their sympathy, but we were all in it together. There may have been the occasional, undercover local delivery of a bottle of wine or two amongst us. I was grateful for that – thank you, anonymous donor ...

"What are you working on so much? How are you keeping busy? You don't even have Netflix, do you?"

I tried to explain what I was doing but it added to my stress. I wouldn't have had time for tv in any case.

I had to stop this naval gazing. I had an income to regenerate and a business to build. I threw myself into it.

I worked from first thing in the morning to last thing at night, designing, writing and building. The threat of my going broke and being stuck here forever was looming and I had to move forwards. I concentrated on reinventing and packaging what I do as a marketable product rather than my just offering training and ghostwriting services.

I couldn't wait to get home to the UK, where I could be closer to my market and have electricity when I needed it. Still, at least lockdown in Cape Town would allow enough time for me to work things out with Shelley, and then everything could go back to normal.

I spent days building a new website, when the power was on.

I designed a six-month course, a number of simple tutorials, structured four books as supporting material and researched the software I'd need to create online courses that could be downloaded.

Still nothing from Shelley.

I brushed up on my sound recording and voice over skills, took on a business coach and started the painful process of facing my 'financial embarrassment' and coming up with a new business plan. A proper, grown up one this time.

It all took weeks – nearly all eight of the initial lockdown. In all that time, there was not a peep from my Bezzer.

Then, my return flight was cancelled.

"I'm not surprised, Josie," said Jules, my school pal and travel expert. "The whole world's shut down. I have no business at all."

"Oh, hell. Jules, I'm so sorry," I could only imagine what she and her partner were going through. Both of them were travel agents, and their income simply stopped. At least I had the opportunity to generate business. "I wish there were something I could do."

She paused. "Actually," she sounded conspiratorial, "maybe there's something you can do."

Jules told me of their plans to get out of the city and move into their holiday rental home, start work on it and prepare it for when the market opened up again.

"That means that our townhouse will be empty." I knew her home – it was stunning, real luxury compared to my one-roomed studio with toxic trees. "And the cats won't have anyone to cuddle ..." she cleverly added.

I was sold. My rental was at an end in any case. If I was to be stuck renting in Cape Town within four walls for potentially months, hers would be perfect.

At last, perhaps I was getting a bit of a break. It was a win-win start to autumn. I could be warm and comfortable, at least.

Fortunately, she lived two kilometers away, so my clandestine move slid smoothly below the radar. I now had a bath, three cats for company, Netflix, a proper office with decent WiFi and a non-toxic garden to nurture me through whatever was going to happen next.

All of this time, Miree was continuing her post-op treatment. She came to the end of her chemo course, weathering it all with grace and positivity. She's a buoyant personality, but this mix of circumstances was enough to bring anybody down.

We found out that she could legally designate me to drive her to and from the hospital for her new radiation appointments if we both wore masks. I did this a few times, relishing the crisp, dark start in the early winter mornings, the snaking along empty roads to her cottage ten minutes away.

Mist swept towards us as we clambered up and over Wynberg Hill toward the hospital. Neither of us mentioned it, but I knew Miree was watching the quietness all around us on the freeway.

How long had it been since the mountain had been silent at this time in the morning? It was all ours, now. For a breath. We could be together, rounding the pine woods of Constantia and Newlands, skirting the suburbs from above, looking out to the ocean, inhaling the scent of Kirstenbosch Gardens, the waterfalls tumbling from Table Mountain with no-one around us until we reached the hospital.

I parked and waited for her, listening to our old radio station for fifteen minutes until she was done.

"Wanna get a coffee?" I offered, as we headed back down Wynberg Hill about a mile from her place. "I need to get some petrol," I excused myself for the unlawful stop.

I wanted time with her, and she wanted it, too, but not to talk. Just to sit, with our take-out coffees in her wide garden, sitting sheltered in our wicker chairs feeling enwrapped by the ferns, blue gum, birdlife, weeds, the years of unkemptness and fun.

Perfect.

"The day will come when you'll be able to leave again, Josie. I don't want you to go," she smiled quietly.

Sitting there with her made me feel as though I didn't want to go, either. Hearing her say that, too, was the tonic my heart needed after the pain of my losing another friendship I thought I could always count on. It was clear that I needed to wish Shelley well, let go of our friendship and move on with my business.

Miree and I talked often about our living with the threat of cancer. I've had five melanoma and have lost both parents to secondary cancer from it. I'm no stranger to that thick clod of fear that burrows into you just below your solar plexus once you've heard the words, "You have cancer."

If you think about it, it shouldn't really be that much of a shock for anyone hearing the news. One in two of us will have cancer at some point in our lives. But that's the thing: fear isn't a 'thinking' thing. It's an instinct, an animal response to threat. Fight, flight or freeze – you are driven to do all three, but in this case none of them gets you anywhere.

The best thing is to know who your friends are and lean on them without apology. And to sit in their garden, sip frothy coffee and laugh at the dog chasing squirrels.

She was right, though. My time had come to go home, at last. With Jules' help, I had managed to secure a last-minute return flight and would be leaving in a week. I faced two weeks' quarantine on landing, and then a move to a little village near Salisbury.

I was desperate to get back to the South West, where I had grown up – a world away from London and Cape Town. I am a country girl at heart. I needed time and space to focus on standing on my own two feet again, personally and business-wise. Over ten months, my world had felt completely out of control. Now, with a little help from my old friends, my business coach and my renewed mindset, I had made decisions that had reinvented my present. I had a business with actual products to market, rather than a service to offer.

As I packed my suitcase, throwing out old boxes of hayfever tablets and mosquito spray, I thought of how the UK had changed since I'd been gone. Ever since COVID-19 had thrown the cat among the pigeons, townies had swarmed to resettle in the beautiful, British countryside. Rumour had it that many were already a bit taken aback by the rawness of country life.

The top gripes that urbanites had with their new homes in the countryside included weak WiFi, rats, unlit roads, stinky manure, potholes, stinging nettles and the lack of burger bars. Oh, and that fuzzy, bindweedy stuff that sticks to your designer jeans.

I just loved all of it. I couldn't wait to go home.

In Spring, the mountainside fairly glitters with an assurance of new life. As we all huddled around log fires and bemoaned the wind and rain, the pine-wooded slopes of Tokai and Constantia quietly began to sparkle and paint fresh colour schemes into the backdrop of a freezing Cape Town. Pale greens, yellows, pinks and blues wove a delicate defence against the last of the winter storms, and everywhere there was a sense of buoyancy and relief.

As I sat at Gate 4 in Cape Town International airport looking out to the Hottentot mountains far beyond the solitary 'plane that stood below me on the tarmac, I prayed my thanks. Thanks for the year I'd had, for my health, for Miree's returning strength, for the opportunity to be with my old friends again, for my old laptop which had bravely fought on and survived, for my new understanding that people can change. Even those whom you think you know inside and out.

Apart of that Eighties ex-cop downstairs at passport control, though. I doubted he'd ever change.

I giggled behind my mask as I realised that that had been the most frightening moment of my entire ten-month adventure. I had been literally five seconds away from being arrested and detained for who knows how long after ten months of entrapment.

If that ex-cop had chosen to go the other way, I wouldn't be writing this today. I'd be stuck somewhere like Robben Island, thinking that the world had gone mad in 2020.

Oh, hang on … it had, hadn't it?

To find out more: jo.collie@authorshipmentorprogramme.co.uk
                                  www.authorshipmentorprogramme.co.uk

KEY 5: COURAGE

There's a difference between tenacity and courage. Both are important to an entrepreneur, but consider the difference:

Tenacity is your ability to hang in there when things get tough.

Courage is your willingness to change things when they get tough.

The fact that you're running your own business or are planning to show that you already have a measure of both. Let's face it, many people never make that leap to starting a business as the risks can be terrifying. How many great ideas are still out there, waiting to be shared with the world? Courage is the characteristic that so many of us feel we lack.

The good news is, though, that it can be developed. It's not something that we were given at birth in greater or lesser degrees. It's something that grows over time and experience – the kinds of experiences you have when you take risks.

Here are two ways you can start to develop yours:

- Take a few minutes to think of small risks you'd like to take – not necessarily with your business at first. It could be a sport, or giving a speech, or dancing in front of an audience like a loon. Give your body and mind an opportunity to feel that rush of adrenaline – however small – every single day. Get used to it, and you'll grow to like it.

- Tell someone about your goals. That way, you become more accountable to your taking action. If you keep them a secret, it lets you off the hook if you don't attain them, as nobody has to know you 'failed'. Take yourself seriously and move forwards.

When you develop your courage, you are able to stand your ground more easily in the face of opposition. Wouldn't it be great to not flinch when that dodgy, shouty client comes along whose work you'd love to turn down?

The more risks of varying intensity you take, the more your courage will develop. Strangely, your tenacity does, equally. Having the courage to stand up to and take on your deepest fear in business is crucial for your welfare and your business's survival.

What is your deepest fear?

Fear of financial ruin affects most of us at some time. While a bit of pressure can be good for momentum and growth, crippling terror is a killer for entrepreneurs.

When Paul found himself on the losing end of a partnership that went horribly wrong, he feared he'd be out on the streets before long. The next story explains how he managed to fight back against his fear by wilfully growing in courage. It's good to know that you can develop it even if you're feeling as fragile as a fragile thing …

Learning to Feel Secure

by Paul Edwards

Interim CRO at Seahorse Automation Limited.
Passionately supporting businesses to deliver ambitious improvements in
revenue, profit and performance.
Guildford, United Kingdom

In life, you're often most successful when you operate from a secure footing. Once, I was placed in a time of uncertainty, by my own actions and those of others. All at a time when the COVID-19 pandemic created an uncertain world and consequently heightened everyone's concern for the future.

That time impacted on me and my friends with whom I had gone into business - the result of other friends' and colleagues' airing their views about the on-going handle I had on my business ... the comments they expressed against the economic backdrop of COVID-19 and, of course, their concern for or interest in my future financial stability.

I learnt to rely on friendship and love over all else. I never lost sight of the danger but instead of worrying about it, prepared for the worst so that I could deliver the best for everyone.

Let me introduce myself:

I had a positive, working class start to life. I had two working parents, until my father died aged forty-eight. I was five at the time, when we were fortunate to move into a new Council house. My mother worked in the local factory for a couple of years and then returned to a position as a matron of a children's home.

Consequently, I saw others struggle with poverty but experienced none myself. Instead, I was brought up to believe in the importance of education and that I should study, graduate from university, from where I could get a good job and expand my horizons past the life expected of a typical working class lad.

This I did, as successfully as many but not as successfully as some. My experience has led me to believe that we are all on some spectrum or another – so we should be tolerant of others, if possible.

Only recently, it was pointed out to me that I have probably lived all my life with 'poverty syndrome'. Not that I am poor, far from it; but that I have lived in fear of being poor. Of ending up on the streets. Internally, I have agreed with that statement and am now working on acts that contradict it.

This is the story of one of those acts.

In 2017, a friend invited me to start a business which he could help operate that built on his experience in the events industry, and knowledge of specialist, high-end, High-Fidelity equipment.

This opportunity was an attractive one and, with a few caveats, I grabbed it with both hands. Thinking it would broaden my experience of managing a fully fledge business and real-life profit and loss (balance sheet, statement of accounts, etc.), which I hoped I may one day be able to utilise as an entrepreneur, investor or M&A advisor in my own right.

My colleague also had demonstrable success as a businessman and entrepreneur. Albeit over thirty years, his efforts have required him to re-invent his business at least a couple of times. That said, I believed that his expertise could only brush off on me, as we would have time to work closely together. Additionally, I considered the learning experience would be beneficial to my corporate career.

Lofty ambitions and goals, then.

Only a few snags:

1. I wasn't quite convinced that entering the high-end, hi-fi market was a good strategy, and this did absorb my start-up investment.

2. Time – mine and that of my friend, to work together.

3. Health!

4. Trust and understanding – mutual, and ...

5. Most importantly… the exit timeframe.

At the very start of the business, I must admit that I was not convinced about the plan to supplement the event production service with a fledgling hi-fi product brand, despite the challenging landscape for the former. However, not wishing to be start the new venture from a negative perspective, I didn't feel I could freely share this concern with my friend.

This omission – effectively an unintentional abdication of responsibility for the business – continued, as plans to meet monthly to review progress quickly fell to quarterly, then half-yearly.

We had only four or five business review meetings within the first year to eighteen months, despite my good intentions.

One reason for this, of course, was my corporate career.

This was where I had developed an unhealthy work ethic, which started from my earliest role as a project engineer before I moved into sales and marketing. It drove me to become a workaholic. My raison d'etre was to generate and deliver sales for my employer, at the expense of my personal ambitions, private life, and time. I was always more stressed about work than daily struggles, which today I recognise as not always a bad thing, yet in all things we benefit from balance. This is something I hope I am learning.

A learning tangent …

Earlier, I mentioned that I consider myself a workaholic as I was always more stressed about work than daily struggles.

Having entered, to a degree, into voluntary retirement in 2020, work became more of a hobby than the necessity I previously perceived it to be. One day, though, in early 2021, I was challenged: I had to take our dog to the vet, fix a broken boiler, a broken-down car and a puncture to the second vehicle all within the space of two to three hours in a morning. And all whilst dealing with decisions around pension transfers and the handling of a complaint with my mobile phone provider.

It was that day I realised that, had I been working, I would have had no alternative but to prioritise which of the incidents to handle first or, in fact, that day and which I would have had to put off and handle on another occasion. It also occurred to me that I was more adept, more capable and less stressed – probably due to my experience – at handling multiple work related incidents and priorities than personal ones. As I say, I am learning to balance varying challenges and to relax.

Tangent ended!

Of course, my friend's desire to drive and operate the business unhindered was another reason we did not meet as often as we planned.

Consequently, this lack of communication resulted in my having serious concerns around my appreciation of the first year accounts and the state of the business and its future potential and trajectory. All of which started to erode my confidence in the business across the board.

It is perhaps surprising, then, that in 2019 when my employer started to communicate that my role as GSI Alliance Director, EMEA, was under threat and it may be subject to redundancy, my first response was to investigate another business partnership. This time in a business that I had once been active. I was excited to hear the past colleagues whom I had encouraged to buy the UK franchise had done exactly that.

Their invitation for me to consider joining them came at a welcome time. It's true to say that we had great ambitions for the partnership and the accelerated revenue I hoped to generate, given my past performance in the space.

Within four months of my joining, however, I realised we had done too little due diligence. Our ambitions were unrealistic. I understood, for the first time, the difference between stepping into a small established business and creating a pipeline within a start-up. In the former, sales time aspirations are reasonably set at fifty to sixty per cent for customer time, and within the latter twenty per cent, is difficult to achieve. During this time I also recognised how much collaboration was important to me to achieve a goal and, despite my being somewhat aloof on occasion, that was the type of environment in which I wished to work.

So, while I was occupied with the above, what was happening to the events and hi-fi business, I hear you ask?

Well, I would like to say that 2018/19 was a breeze. It was not. Predominantly because my friend, who was excessively overweight, started to have serious health problems. In addition to hypertension, which is perhaps not unexpected in a man of over fifty-five who had been a relatively successful entrepreneur and enjoyed the good things for most of his life, he started to suffer heart failure. His heart was operating at less than twenty-five per cent capacity at various points.

Despite this, he continued to operate the event side of the business successfully and grow the specialist hi-fi product business. However, the second year trading showed high cost of sale and insufficient margin. This heightened my concerns as to the business's long-term viability and its ability (and that of my friend) to recoup my investment in it. This was important from my perspective as my own monthly income looked to be in jeopardy,

I entered the pandemic very much one of the lost three million in the UK with no income and no means to secure any personal financial relief or support. That said, I felt perhaps for the first time in my career that my destiny was in my own hands. I started to explore whether and how the assets I had amassed during my working career - various pensions, investments, etc. - might be sufficient to allow me to act as if I were retired. Even so, my ambition was to explore an alternative way of working and/or of generating income.

Critically, to finance the gap between from that point and to one where I could realistically realise other forms of income, I needed the business I owned to return my investment in line with the initial three-year exit plan we had envisaged at its inception. The most viable option for this always had been the instance of my selling the business to my friend. So, I started to press for how we might achieve this given the circumstances.

I started to become distressed about the commitment to the sale and the heightened risk in the operation of the business. I sought advice from a friend with much greater experience than I. Sharing the first- and second-year statement of accounts over a curry, it was he who highlighted the high cost of sale, pointed me to where I should actually be raising questions in relation to what the accounts suggested and kindly furnished me with a few appropriate, probing questions to ask. He knew that I was in business with my friend and was mindful that there were other forces at play which meant an ultra-critical review of the business was inappropriate.

It was clear, though, that cash was not readily available to support the proposed transfer and maintain the ongoing investment needed by the business.

Consequently, a few actions were necessary:

1. To survive, the business needed to take a firm position on the letter of our contracts for event service deliverable which were impacted by COVID-19. Our customers would be required to pay according to the contract and, where necessary, invoke their insurance against their having to cancel. At the same time, wherever possible we should cancel at no charge any third-party services we planned to use and which were no longer needed.

2. Pivot the niche face-to-face sales and marketing approach we had adopted to promote the high-fidelity business to one of an interactive online model.

3. Secure all the pandemic related grants and loans available and appropriate to the business.

However, whilst in the most part these were all completed successfully, my friend was still reluctant to progress the transfer of the business. We discussed and agreed alternative ways to finance the transfer on which he reneged.

A perfect storm ensued: I attended some business training which taught me a number of things I lacked about the financials and structuring of a business; I started to explore entering into a partnership of a start-up; at the same time, I believed it important to take some legal advice about my current business and did so.

It was at this point too that I started to employ an approach I had used extensively in my corporate life. I began documenting every discussion and agreed strategy. I sent this following a meeting, asking for written acknowledgement or comment. I effectively used the correspondence as unsigned contracts which, if not adhered too, at least required an explanation. This naturally led to the construction of a revised agreement until the desired outcome was successfully completed. I wasn't shy to include influencers in the correspondence, or arguments conveying appropriate amounts of power.

The elements of my perfect storm brought me confidence, consternation and an appreciation of the process of successfully selling and transferring a business in equal measure:

- The training brought about confidence regarding to the framework of the business and my ownership of it, including the importance of critical IP, customer data, trademarks, websites etc.

- My exploration of a new start-up partnership raised concerns about the trust I had in the people involved in my other business. These, I later realised, were unfounded or too exaggerated in my case. That said, as a consequence, I have adopted a philosophy that I would like to adhere to for the rest of my working life, if I can: "Wherever possible, do business with people you like, whether they be customers, suppliers, employees or partners. Whilst, understanding that this won't stop you falling out from time to time, it should make life easier and ensure you resolve issues more quickly – which, after all is the heart of every business – and therefore make you and everyone more successful."

- While disappointment still may come, it will at least be easier to deal with because it should be a shared experience.

- My astute commercial solicitor's providing a clear understanding of the process of selling a company and other complications. She clearly outlined the options from what was necessary to dot every 'i' and cross every 't'. She then also outlined more pragmatic approaches which I used, discussing in a calm and professional manner the risks of taking a more trusting approach to a company transfer based on its value and the understanding that existed between the parties involved.

Hindered by the consternation generated by some of the above and armed with just as much valuable advice, I re-engaged numerous times with my friend to progress the company sale.

The first time, it was to agree the contract payments that would be used to enable the transfer. These were spent by the business without my knowledge.

The second time, it was to discuss and discount the use of 'bounce' bank loans – it's prohibited.

The third time, we discussed our mutually funding the ongoing business under his stewardship, using his funds to return my initial investment. His funds were ultimately transferred into another venture.

I was upset and was issued a small prescription of hypertension medication. I used my documentation of the past months' discussions and failed actions to try to press home the need for an immediate resolution.

The consequence of this not what I expected as my friend effectively transferred the business to his alternative company venture – lock stock and barrel (stock, IP, etc.).

That was an "Oh, shit!" moment.

As we engaged for a fourth time, it became clear that he had no ulterior motive or malicious intention for doing this. He was just afraid for his own livelihood, just as I had concerns for mine. The transparent nature of the conversation we had that time around was, I feel, due to my honest documentation of what had transpired and how I felt about it. It was only made possible because I had captured our conversations as they had occurred. This correspondence allowed him to open up about his concerns and fears, too.

Our fourth plan was hatched in which we discussed the appointment of a financial guarantor to enable the sale. This was difficult for him, but we discussed and agreed what the contractual paperwork should look like and set up a meeting with our accountant and one of their senior partners to discuss the proposal. This advice was paid for by my friend using my accountant.

Finally, the transfer was completed successfully in March 2021. Interestingly though, the night before we planned to proceed, it was I who changed his mind.

I remembered why I had invested in the company in the first place and my overarching goals. They were, for the most part, for the sake of our friendship. I had been aware of the risks and of the benefits. It was my uncertainty that had led to me to worry about the eventual outcome.

I was now certain about what mattered: it was our friendship - not the business.

I took action against my "poverty syndrome". We completed the transfer of the business for £1 and I trusted that my friend would find a way of returning my monies in the wash – which he did.

Today, I am grateful for friendship and that if I suffer it is with a syndrome, not poverty which should be everyone's concern.

To find out more: paul.edwards@robgoddard.co.uk
                      www.robgoddard.co.uk

KEY 6: CHALLENGE

It's a cruel irony that we need a bit of discomfort in our lives to learn how to become the best version of ourselves. I mean, who wants challenges? A life of peace and quiet sounds far more appealing.

Challenges are actually healthy for us, though. We need challenge to benefit our business and personal lives. Here are a few ways you can benefit from challenge:

- It helps you figure out what it is you really want. There's nothing like a bit of dissatisfaction to make you dream of a more ideal situation. Motivation to improve things comes naturally when you're challenged.

- It teaches you gratitude – a very important lesson in business. As Joni Mitchell sang, "Don't it always seem to go that you don't know what you got till it's gone ..." (Big Yellow Taxi, from the album "Ladies of the Canyon", 1970), sometimes we need to lose something to make us re-evaluate it. If you've experienced this, hopefully you'll get it back again soon.

- It shows you how tough you can be. Coming through an ordeal and landing safely on the other side is a brilliant way to discover your own inner strength. We usually underestimate ourselves, only to find how resilient and resourceful we can be when we're put under pressure.

- It gives the taste of success a memorable sweetness. When was the last time you struggled against the odds to achieve a goal? Can you remember how fulfilled you felt afterwards? Without the challenge, your life would be pretty dull.

- Repeated challenge is excellent fuel for growing your tenacity and courage (more on that later). You need a lot of grit and determination in business; challenge is the best way to get more of it.

The really good news is that, if you're running your own business, you won't have to wait long or look too far to find a challenge or two. They come along uninvited, most of the time, rudely gatecrashing your life when you least want them.

When Marc took a risk and dramatically changed his role within his company, he really had to step up to the momentous challenge of changing the way it operated from the top down. He dug deep … here is his story of how he rose to his challenge and how he made his young son proud.

Standing On The Shoulders of Giants

by Marc Maurer

Portfolio Manager at Volaris Group
Zurich, Switzerland

The news struck me with a combination of surprise and uncertainty. Did he just say that he wants to resign from his role as managing director?

I took a deep breath and grabbed a seat.

Here I was, nine months into the completed acquisition of this niche software company. It was a challenging ride with lots of back-and-forth discussions, raising tensions between the managing director and me, and multiple moments when I thought I could see some light in the tunnel where our relationship moved. But eventually, every spark of hope that he would fix the business for good was nipped in the bud.

I leant back and closed my eyes for a minute or two and all the pictures and impressions of the last eighteen months reappeared before my mind's eye.

The Big Opportunity

John contacted me in May 2018, and it was a dream come true. It was my fourth year as M&A Director at Volaris, a large conglomerate consisting of hundreds of software companies.

I joined the group with no prior M&A experience; rather, I had held many sales roles in software and technology businesses. This background of selling and relationship building convinced Volaris to move me into the M&A role. It was my ability to build relationships with people quickly that allowed me to acquire several vertical market software businesses in Germany and Switzerland.

I reframed the buying companies process in selling alternative futures to business owners. I learned about the stories of their companies, about their challenges and hopes so that I could connect them with what we can offer as a new owner. It was a truly rewarding experience.

Still, I was always interested in the operational side as well. After the acquisition came another acquisition, always. I imagined that spending more time with the teams to help them practically to move their companies to a next level must be interesting, too.

In mid-2017, I started talking to various people about my wish to eventually build up an own portfolio of companies. It was a path nobody had walked before as the internal pre-requisite for the role of a portfolio manager is a strong track of record in running software businesses. I have led sales teams in the past but never wore the hat of a managing director.

At the beginning of 2018, however, Volaris started to decentralize their M&A practice. This meant that portfolio leaders like John needed to not only build up new M&A teams but to acquire companies on their own, fast. From John's point of view, I could ensure a fast track to acquisitions and he was able to coach me on integrating these companies. A good fit and my shortcut to portfolio manager while skipping the operational route completely, so I thought.

The first couple of months as portfolio manager without a portfolio went by in the same way as the three years before.

In the late summer of 2018, I was reading a book on our patio when

Aaron, one of our three children, was playing tabletop football against one of his schoolmates. Aaron was seven-years old by that time and he always fascinated me with his ability to think on his feet.

"So, what does your dad do?" Asked his friend.

Aaron responded casually, "It's a complicated job."

"What do you mean?"

"He's buying companies for Volaris."

This impressed the lad. "A whole company?" he squeaked. "Really?

"Yes," said Aaron, shrugging. "It's like eBay."

I smiled. But I also was thinking that my job description would become even more complicated once I bought the first company for my own portfolio. I had to wait until March 2019. As I signed the sales purchase agreement with a power of attorney from Volaris it indeed felt different compared to the other times I did this. This company I had to integrate myself. I was not in Kansas anymore.

Trials and Challenges

Acquiring this business was not easy. The company was in the middle of a technology rewrite and the business case required a few changes of its strategy. I had to meet our investment committee three times, refining the plan again and again. I remained confident that the current Managing Director was open to change.

Eventually, though, after I signed the sales purchase agreement, we soon held the townhall meeting to inform the employees about the acquisition.

And then the real work began.

It soon turned out that my perception of the Managing Director being coachable was wrong. Although we aligned on the main points of the integration plan beforehand, he thought to convince me to run the business as he did before. Of course, I did not allow it but tried to re-convince him of the plan.

This tug-of-war obviously damaged the business. It went on for six months. John provided good advice along the way but insisted that I should make my own decisions. I wondered a few times if I should fire the Managing Director but always found reasons not to. He was too important for delivering the integration plan, what would the employees and clients think, maybe he just needed time to adapt ...

And then I faced my biggest monster: the Volaris talent reviews came up.

Each autumn, Volaris holds talent reviews where top management reviews the progress, performance, and development of key individuals in our companies. For the first time since I joined Volaris, I did not get an A-grade. I somehow knew this was coming because a big part of the review is my year-to-date performance, which was under pressure because of the losses accumulated by my first portfolio company. But to get a C-grade in the review was a blow to me.

In my role as M&A Director, I reported to Jim. He was also present during the reviews and tried to calm me down. Jim is a very humble person and probably one of the finest souls I encountered during my work life so far. I remember many instances when, in retrospect, his advice was spot on. He mentioned to me that the business case was complex from the beginning, and everybody would have struggled to manage this. The recommendation from the talent reviews were that I should accumulate operational experience.

I was still dissecting this feedback in the back of my mind that day when I entered the office of the Managing Director to discuss the business's future strategy.

A Walk that Reframes Everything

I sit down trying to listen to the reasons why he decided to resign from the role. Honestly, I can't really concentrate on what he says as my mind is racing. What is next? Can I convince him to stay? Should I convince him to stay? Who can overtake the leadership role if he leaves for real? What will staff say when they learn about this? A lot of questions and not a clear line of sight.

I say something like "I understand, let's work this out in a constructive way, I accept your resignation, and meet next week to sort out the logistics. "

As I walk out of the meeting room, I take a deep breath. I need to take a walk outside of the office. That helps me slowing down my racing mind. It's a cold December day but this is good as the chilly atmosphere sharpens my senses for what has to come. Taking a walk usually helps me to see through challenging situations.

So, I ask my three power questions:

• What is life trying to teach me?

• What is the positive element of what just happened?

• What now?

These questions are a true treasure as they are a sure-fire way to reframe every curveball life throws at me. This one is no exception.

Clearly, Life is trying to teach me to be prepared for such situations. My role is that of a portfolio manager and it is my duty to prepare a plan for the scenario that one of my leaders would leave the boat. I want also that my leaders have such plans for when their managers leave. But how can I expect that if such things come to me as a surprise?

And what about the positive elements of the Managing Director leaving? First, isn't it a fact that whoever takes over his position will be better suited to fill out the role in a way I like it? Second, there won't be these heated moments of unproductive arguments anymore, right? And third, staff will not have to endure the disconnect between me and him anymore.

As I walk through a dark underground passage a few hundred meters away from the office it becomes clear what is next. This is the perfect opportunity for me to become operational!

As I walk back into the office, I pick up the phone to call John.

"Hey John, it finally happened," I announce. "The Managing Director just resigned."

A moment's pause. "Oh, really? How do you feel now?"

"Well, after a walk in the cold not too bad," I joke. "Maybe this is rather an opportunity than a crisis."

"How is that?" John doesn't sound convinced.

"It allows me to take over the business and get some operational experience under my belt. Just following the recommendation from the talent reviews. Don't you think?"

I wait while he considers.

"You're right," he says after a moment. "This is a great idea. Let's use the time over Christmas to discuss a plan to turn the company around."

I hang up the phone. Looks like I just promoted myself to become a Managing Director for the first time of my life!

In the evening, I tell my family about the resignation event and what it means for me in terms of the new operational role. They're happy about this turn of events, and Aaron has a question.

"Dad, have you been the boss of a company before? Is it difficult to do?"

I respond honestly. "No, I haven't, and I will need to see how difficult it will be."

This seems good enough for Aaron. Is it for me?

Over the next couple of days, the operational challenge was pushed into the background as the usual before-Christmas hecticness took our lives under autopilot. It was only on December 26th when I found some time to invest in some forecasting of the business - usually a helpful starting point to form a strategy.

I wasn't surprised that there were some significant changes that needed to happen as the company had accumulated a large loss in the year that had just elapsed. A perfect storm had been forming.

Firstly, the company was making too large an investment in a rewrite of its technology by having not one but two external development teams on its payroll. Secondly, the company operated in a 'crowding out' competition in a very small niche, which made winning new clients a very rare event. Indeed, the last time the company won a new client was more than five years ago. Thirdly, the number of professional services projects demanded by existing clients decreased year by year as the time of new implementation projects was long gone.

So, what should I do now to solve this challenge? Maybe the answer to Aaron's question was not that easy after all!

From Plan to Execution

On paper, it was not complicated. I knew what to do. We had too many resources in the business given the current backlog of orders and the immediate outlook of new projects. We also suffered from having two external development teams on the payroll. This created unnecessary costs and a large burden to carry on.

I calculated that I needed to let go of two project managers and to eliminate one of the two development teams. I knew that this is the right thing to do as Volaris used a sophisticated set of ratios that help determining the right level of investment for the various departments.

Looking at these numbers, I felt like I was sitting on the shoulders of a giant as these ratios gave me confidence to do the right thing. They had been created by comparing hundreds of software businesses over years and years. For me, they replaced decades of experience and allow me to shape a solid plan of what to do.

But at that moment, these were just numbers sitting in a spreadsheet. I figured that I needed to tell a good story to both the regular staff and the leadership team at the company. This would be especially important because my decisions affect people.

Most of the assets in a software company are the brains of some highly talented individuals. There is no heavy metal machinery or an inventory full of valuable materials. It's people.

And people get influenced by stories.

This evening, I sit together with Aaron to tell him a bedtime story. He likes listening, like I do. I think it is because it activates his imagination. He is reading a lot of books on his own and often listens to the radio after turning off the lights. I finish the story and close the book.

"Aaron, I noticed that you like to listen to stories, is that right?"

"Yes," he responds, sleepily.

"Why do you think you like listening to stories?"

He frowns a little. "Huh? I don't know. Just like them. They're fun."

It's an honest response and maybe one that is true for all of us. We can't really explain why we are drawn to stories. But maybe it is this unconscious effect stories have on us. We put down our critical filters and are more open if we receive input in the form of a story. This is what I need for my company; a story that pulls us forward into a more positive future.

Soon after the New Year started, I called for a Town Hall meeting so that the managing director and I could inform the employees about his decision to leave the business and that I would take over for the time being. I complimented him for all the good things he had done for the business. He kind of returned the favor by offering a book as a present – "Managing a Business for Dummies". I responded with a smile, saying that I need every help to fill the large gap he leaves behind.

Some of the employees shared later with me that they had not been surprised about the managing director's decision. It was a known fact that "something had to happen".

I didn't want to lose time, so I set up my first leadership team meeting for the next day to share my story with the team leaders.

It was a simple story. First, a diagram that showed our forecast by three lines; net revenues, operational expenditures, and EBITA. This gave evidence that we were hovering around break-even for the year. Second, a bar chart that compared our capacity to do projects versus our backlog of orders, big capacity bars versus small order bars. And a third slide showing my conclusions:

- Remove two project managers

- Shut down one of the two development teams

- Reorganisation of the work to cope without the people leaving

The team accepted the plan but not with clapping hands. The main thing for them was the decision to let the two project managers go. They were good people and they had done nothing wrong. I agreed with them, saying that they were right, these were good people. But at the same time, we could not have a healthy business if we don't reduce the costs. A healthy business is a pre-requisite for a growing business.

This discussion with my leadership team was a good training ground for the communication with the two project managers that needed to follow. We informed them one week later and just before we informed the rest of the staff in a second Town Hall meeting.

One of the two managers took this message in a very constructive way and showed understanding of my decision. The other behaved in a completely different way. After I shared with him that we needed to let him go, he became very emotional and could not understand that he needed to leave despite that fact that he had done nothing wrong.

"What did I do wrong? Why are you letting me go?"

I felt for him. "It is not your mistake," I tried to assure him. "It's the situation that demands action."

"But I really don't understand. I didn't do anything wrong."

This was not how I wanted the conversation to go. "I know, and I understand that this is difficult for you. Please take the rest of the day off and we talk again tomorrow morning," I told him.

It was obvious, my story didn't work for him. It was not his story. He was not part of the story anymore.

The next day, though, he was a different person. We had a much more calm and constructive discussion. I wondered what changed his mind from one day to the other. I have never been made redundant, but I realise that different people deal in different ways with such information.

Onward and Upward

In the Town Hall with the remaining employees, I extended my three slides to provide the team with a richer story. There were two main additions: why we needed to align our vectors and an explanation of why they are important to me.

Vector alignment refers to the idea that everybody in a business can be seen as a vector. As such we have a direction and an impact. In an ideal world, these vectors are aligned and move in the right direction. In a less ideal (or more realistic) world, the vectors are pointing in different directions.

I told the team that now that we had lost some of our colleagues it was important that we aligned ourselves. This meant that some of us had to do things other than what we were used to. An administrative person needed to do some project work. A technical integration person needed to engage in customer support. We needed to reorganize ourselves so that we could move the ship forward.

I also introduced each employee with a photo and explained publicly why I thought that they were important for the business from then on.

Soon after we started working in the new set-up, the global COVID-19 crisis spread around the world. I felt good that I had the necessary changes already at the beginning of the year as my software business showed great perseverance in the face of the pandemic. No customers left us; some of them even gave us even additional orders. I am grateful that we started the year with a conservative plan.

It's the end of the year and I gather the team in front of our office with the appropriate virus-compliant distancing.

"I am very thankful that all of you moved outside of your comfort zone to keep or ship not only afloat but that we could travel a great distance. We did not only grow the business quite a bit — we're up twenty-five per cent - but we managed to do it with some very good profitability."

As I return home that evening, I tell Aaron after his bedtime story about what happened.

" The employees have been very proud as I mentioned the business results, Aaron," I smile.

"What was your part in this, Dad?"

I'm glad he's asked. "Well, I think I decided the changes and communicated them to the employees. Then the employees were very helpful to each other, and they achieved more as a result. If people help each other, good things happen, Aaron."

As he closes his eyes later, I conclude that there are two transformations happening this year. Firstly, the company has become healthier and staff are working better together as a result of it. Secondly, I have experienced a personal transformation.

I learned from the giants in the form of the Volaris ratios and best practices. They infused me with confidence so that I could act as Managing Director.

This experience has definitely changed me and will help me for what is yet to come.

To find out more: marc.maurer@volarisgroup.com
                      www.volrarisgroup.com

KEY 7: FLEXIBILITY

There is a type of person in the business world who holds back from developing new ways of thinking, who stays stuck in the mud with an inflexible mindset. The problem is, the business gets stuck in the mud, too.

This kind of person sees constructive criticism as a personal attack, rather than a chance to improve, obstacles as a reason to give up rather than an opportunity to find a solution. They're far less likely to take calculated risks.

Usually, a person with an inflexible mindset doesn't believe that a person can change – develop a new talent or view things in a different way. It's true that adopting a 'growth mindset' as someone who's run a business for long time with a 'fixed' one is very difficult. You rarely see it. It is possible to do, though.

If you think you might need a more flexible approach to your business and decision making, here are some points to get you loosened up:

- Allow yourself to feel discomfort when you try new things; anything new takes time to become a habit

- Notice and acknowledge your weak points, learn what is there for you to work on. You might ask someone you trust for some honest appraisal to help you – just don't take what they say personally!

- Shift your focus from the outcome to the process itself, for example, from the sales revenue to the client relationship building

- Learn to view obstacles as opportunities to find solutions, exercising that fabulous brain of yours in some lateral thinking

- Success will eventually follow 'failure', so don't throw in the towel too early

- Take constructive criticism as helpful advice, not a personal attack. If you can learn to welcome it, you'll change positively much more quickly and make new friends, too

Read on to find out how Colin discovered that flexibility was key to his taking the next step with his business. After a little hesitation, he listened to the rest of our coaching group and tried out what they challenged him to do. It made quite an impact on his sales ... let alone his way of thinking!

How I Got Out Of My Own Way

by Colin Newbold

Transforming Leadership and Management Capability Through Novel
360-Degree Feedback Methodologies
Bells Yew Green, United Kingdom

I'm the CEO of a micro-business specialising in 360-degree feedback. Prior to this, I was involved in the development of leaders and managers, both as a facilitator of classroom-based training workshops and as a leadership coach to teams and individuals.

I wasn't always in the learning and development profession, my early career was in pharmaceuticals and spanned many years. I worked my way up from a medical representative for an international drug company, through a marketing role within the same company and finally rose to the giddy heights of national sales manager.

To quote one of my favourite authors, the late Stephen Covey, "As I continued climbing the career ladder I slowly realised that it was up against the wrong wall." It was as I neared the top that I realised my real passion lay in the development of human potential, particularly managers and leaders. I started as an independent trainer in 1987 and formed The Learning Curve (TLC) in 1991.

I later developed an interest in one of the most widely-used resources in leadership and management development and set up TLC Online to specialise in the provision of 360-degree feedback to small, medium and large-sized organisations across the globe.

360 feedback (or 'multi-rater feedback' as it is sometimes known) is a popular questionnaire-based resource for developing leaders and managers. As the person receiving the 360, you invite a group of colleagues that work around you to complete a short questionnaire on your capabilities. You also complete the questionnaire from your own perspective. The report that comes out at the end compares your self-perceptions against those of your colleagues, thereby showcasing your strengths as well as areas for development. It is based on the premise that 'how you see yourself is all very well, but it is how others see you that will likely determine the results you get.'

My TLC Online business is several years old. We started trading in the late 1990s and I have kept the business lean and mean ever since. By 2020, as the coronavirus started to gather momentum and sweep across the globe, business began to slow down with the consequence that I had more time to reflect on more fundamental strategic issues.

During the pandemic, I was invited to join an international co-coaching group founded by serial entrepreneur Rob Goddard. The sessions were to be virtual via the online meeting platform Zoom. The group was made up of senior managers from several different countries, most of them running their own businesses in a diverse variety of industry sectors.

Anyone who has started a micro-business will know that it can get very lonely at the top. More importantly, it can be difficult to make sound, well-judged decisions when there are no other senior managers to bounce ideas off. Sounding boards, if they exist at all, tend to be outside the business, typically not knowledgeable about the business and not necessarily helpful. Here was an opportunity to join a like-minded bunch of similar others for support and encouragement.

I didn't expect the other group members to know much about my world of 360-degree feedback (one of them later commented that it took 2 sessions before she could understand what I was talking about!), but from the way Rob described them I did expect them to be supportive. In addition, I really thought I could contribute some of my own wisdom as well as learning from theirs.

The structure of the monthly group sessions meant that during each meeting two of us had an opportunity to present a problem that we invited the other group members to discuss. We hoped in this process that the group would offer ideas and encouragement. "A problem shared is a problem halved", as they say.

When it came to my turn, I decided to take the challenge of reinventing my pricing mechanisms to the group and ask for their help in coming up with an easier, more competitive way of charging. For some time before the group started, I had realised that our pricing model, with ten decreasing price bands based on increasing volumes, was dated and neither clear, straightforward, nor competitive. However, this was a pricing model that I had spent many hours developing and finally brought into the world. It was a pricing model that I was justifiably (understandably) proud of and wedded to. It had served me well up to this point and, using the old adage "If it ain't broke, don't fix it", I was finding it hard to let go of. On the other hand, I had lost several pitches over the last few years because of price and I was aware that my pricing mechanism was overly complicated.

The reception that I received from the group was overwhelming in its focus: do away with the 'per report' cost and just go with a simple tiered banding…as an example for the enterprise offering: bundle in the reports and just charge for the site build, the hosting and the support. Three tiers would allow for small, medium and large implementations.

Their suggestion was a radical departure from what I had been used to for twenty years and I noticed how resistant I suddenly felt. Without meaning to be, I think I was quite rude in my response at the time, saying something like 'it will never work, that's not how we do things'. In fact, I could feel a sense of anger inside, it was almost like these guys were attacking my child. They just didn't get it…the world they operate in is just so different.

Having written that, it is also fair to admit that even at the time I was recognising a pattern in my psychology which is associated with the need to be right. Don't we all feel that way? A little bit? I was probably sounding arrogant to the other group members. It wouldn't be the first time I'd been thought of as arrogant and although none of us consciously wants to be seen that way, I suspect our passion blinds us sometimes from what others see.

My own psychology can be best illustrated by an incident that happened during my time in the Army Cadets whilst at Highgate School in North London. Although only a young nipper, I clearly remember marching with the other Cadets round and round the playing field and my commanding officer shouting out my name followed by the words "You're out of step boy!". Quick as anything I replied "No, I'm not, sir, they are".

On another occasion, much later in my life, I took up motor racing with the genuine belief that I would be challenging for the win after just a few races. How wrong was I!

In my first race, on the hallowed international GP track at Silverstone, my car failed to get through scrutineering due to my misunderstanding the rule book. I managed to get a special dispensation from the Clerk of the Course, just so that I could qualify, and I then had about four hours before the race to fix the problem.

I managed this with just seconds to go, but I had missed the assembly area and I had to join the race from the pit lane. In actual fact, I could neither find my way to the assembly area (behind the Medical Centre at Silverstone) nor could I see a way through to the pit lane! I finally got on track and then once there – this is my first ever motor race you understand – I couldn't work out whether the race had started or not. Were they still on the 'green flag' lap? When I saw in my mirrors a gaggle of the leading cars bearing down on me, like a bunch of enemy fighter planes in the Battle of Britain, it was all I could do just to stay out of their way.

Needless to say, I came plumb last in that race! Hugely damaging to my fragile ego. Thankfully I improved throughout the year and ended up with the 'Novice of the Year' trophy!

That night I went to bed with my head full of reasons why this simplified pricing model would not work. I slept really badly, waking up several times with anxiety born out of frustration with my colleagues.

Eventually I was able to let things go and woke up the next morning feeling tired but resolute. I decided to book a call with the group leader and talk through all the reasons why their pricing model wouldn't work.

Rob was defiant in his defence of the group's idea. As hard as I pushed, so he pushed back. I felt we had truly reached an impasse. Despite that, we ended the call amicably and I resolved to carry on thinking up different ways to improve the pricing model. Now, it felt like I was in a competitive battle to prove Rob and the group wrong. Every way I looked at it, I couldn't see how we could let go of the 'per report' pricing element. I had to be right. I thought about testing some ideas with my best clients but in my conversation with Rob he had warned me against that.

I left the challenge of inventing a new pricing mechanism alone for a few days while I concentrated on business as usual. At least by now, April 2021, business was slowly starting to pick up.

Then suddenly, about a week after I'd brought the problem to the group, I had one of those 'lightbulb moments'. It suddenly dawned on me...there might be a way to take the best of the group's suggestions and yet not make a complete departure from what had gone before.

What better way to discover if this would be acceptable to current clients than to test it?

I decided to try it out on one of our established clients, Mercer. At the time that this pricing challenge was going on, we were engaged in the scoping and costing of a brand new application for one of their customers: TowerBrook, a fintech firm.

Only days before, I had put a price to my main contact at Mercer which had been based on the old model and that had been accepted. I was about to generate a Work Order (WO) for signing when I now went back with the new pricing model which would cost them slightly more each month.

Needless to say, my client contact pushed back very hard and in the end I had to concede some ground but the important outcome was that Mercer accepted the new pricing model at the Tier 1 level and signed off my WO. It had worked!

Now it was time to test the new model on another major client and that worked even better! At the time of presenting the new enterprise pricing model to them there were only three tiers. But after talking through the high number of reports they were projecting for the future, my client helped me to realise that I'd priced it too low!

I hastily made up a story that I was working on a fourth tier and would get back to them shortly with what that looked like.

They were happy with Tier 4 and signed off the new contract accordingly.

Suddenly, it started to dawn on me that the problem was more in my head than in the clients'. A few weeks later, I had successfully converted a prospect to a customer using the new model. What is more, during the six weeks between April and May, I converted two more prospects using the new model and was able to successfully renegotiate an acceptance of the new pricing with an existing customer. It is now my established pricing mechanism.

So, what learning do I take from this valuable experience?

1) We are our own worst enemy, frequently getting in our own way. What happened to me in this story is that my company had adopted a pricing mechanism, mainly of my making, that had originally been influenced by the pricing mechanisms of those competitors against whom I'd benchmarked myself in the start-up days. Over the years, I had conducted further research to check if that's how everybody else was still doing it. One time I even commissioned Patrick, one of my own coaches, to pose as a mystery shopper and ask for quotes from the major players at the time.

"Don't reveal your association with me and TLC Online," I had stressed, "and see if you can get to see their questionnaire interfaces and their reports at the same time."

These days, much more of that information is available via the internet and even competitor websites seem to reveal a lot more information than they did. To be honest, one of the disappointing outcomes of that research is how different everybody's pricing seemed to be at the time, although there tends to be general parity these days around the costs for a single 360 feedback report.

I even approached a couple of competitor companies in more recent years, ostensibly with a view to possible collaborations, but I was careful to note what products and services they were offering and at what prices.

Looking at my own psychology in all of this, I can clearly see now how I was looking for evidence that justified and supported – defended, even – my own pricing mechanism at the time. I think I had actually developed a 'scotoma' (a blind spot) to pricing mechanisms that were out of sync with our own.

I have discovered through this and other experiences a dangerous flaw in our psychology: often, being right is more important than being open and sensible. Not a great look. The sad thing for me, reflecting as I write these words, this was a relatively recent occurrence.

Will I never learn?

When all around me are convinced there's a better way, truly listen to their perspectives and don't bring down the shutters straight away. Further reflection, without the spectre of defending and justifying my past behaviour, freed up my mind to allow in new possibilities.

2) A problem shared is a problem halved. Yeah, I know - it's an old cliché but in this case it truly worked. Being the leader of a micro-sized business can be tough and lonely at times and decision-making can be a little off. In my case, I can see now how a level of arrogance had built up over the years to the point where I would go through the motions of sharing my problems with others but all the while desperately clinging on to my old ways.

For example, my ex-wife and I once commissioned a business coach to come into our business and then I spent most of the £1500 per day fee arguing with him about why his ideas wouldn't work. Somewhere in the back of my mind I was replaying that old George Bernard Shaw quote: "Those who can, do. Those who can't, teach."

By belonging to a network of similar others, like the Rob Goddard co-coaching group (people who were "doing", not "teaching"), I opened myself up to enable other perspectives, which appeared radical and unworkable at first, to enter my frame of reference.

3) Test your new ideas on your clients and prospects. That's exactly what I did but as you can see I was counselled by Rob and my fellow group members to tread very carefully when doing this. It could have gone horribly wrong and cost me the clients. At the same time, it might have appeared that I didn't know what I was doing. This is almost certainly easier if the clients and prospects can clearly see a win in it for them but as my story shows there was at least one where the change was going to cost them more. I felt justified in the test once I had thought through the pricing mechanism to a high degree and felt that I could easily defend and justify it.

Often, the resistance is in your own head and not theirs. After all, prospects often don't know any different! At the same time, be receptive to feedback from clients – you never know it may well improve the result, as in my example.

4)   Be open to change. My experience, this story, is ultimately about my resistance to change. My inability to do what Adam Grant, Wharton Professor of Organizational Psychology, calls 'Rethink'. What Rob did that day in his phone call to me was use a technique called 'motivational interviewing' (also referred to as 'Appreciative Enquiry').

To quote Adam Grant, "In motivational interviewing, there's a distinction between sustain talk and change talk. Sustain talk is commentary about maintaining the status quo. Change talk is referencing a desire, ability, need, or commitment to make adjustments."

When contemplating a change, many people are ambivalent – they have some reasons to consider it but also some reasons to stay the course. Two business psychologists that Adam Grant refers to in his book, Miller and Rollnick, suggest asking about and listening for change talk and then posing some questions about how they might change.

"What do you appreciate most about your current pricing mechanism?" Rob asked me.

"It seems fair," I considered. "Prospects and customers respect that it rewards greater volumes with lower prices. The problem is, they find it complicated. There are too many 'pricing bands' – about ten in total."

It didn't take him long to come up with a new suggestion.

"Why not do away with the reports element altogether and just reward them with lower prices in fewer bands? Three or four tiers instead of ten bands."

Rob went on to summarise what three or four tiers could look like, compared with ten bands, and for the first time I had to admit the simplicity was magic. And I thought I was a really open individual, that change was a constant and inevitable!

Truly, I believed that I was a person who welcomed change. Yet, looking back, I can see how much of a dinosaur I must have appeared to Rob and my co-coaching colleagues.

To find out more: cpn@click-360.com
                      www.click-360.com

KEY 8: REBELLION

Without the rebels of this world, we wouldn't have progressed as a species. Our leaders have been rebels, our business giants have begun with rebellious ideas and our different world faiths have been championed by rebels through the ages.

The business world needs more rebels. I'm not talking about the James Dean types, or vigilantes necessarily … I'm talking about you and I, seemingly normal people who have a vision that needs realising. You need a rebel mindset to succeed in entrepreneurship: one which resists convention or tradition when necessary.

One which believes in creativity and innovation.

It's praiseworthy to be able to improve on someone else's idea; if you can think up something brand new that people need, you're a rebel with a cause. There's a new phrase that's bandied about these days to describe you: "constructive deviant". How good does that sound?

You need to be a bit of a rebel by nature to be creative and innovative. If you consider how Apple Macintosh began, you can see that the minds behind it all were rebellious, eager to buck the system and break some rules.

Of course, it doesn't do well to break rules wherever they exist. Clever risk-taking business owners pick their battles, put their creative energies into projects and processes that will measurably help them attain their top goal.

Do you feel you're up to the 'rebel' label? Are you a constructive deviant? If you are, then running your own business is probably a much happier situation for you than working as an employee. Most managers try desperately to stomp out rebellious antics the moment they flare up in the workplace.

If you feel like you could use a little more rebellious energy, though, you can always drum some up. The key to it is finding a cause that really makes your boat float – something that genuinely matters to you. When you feel the frustration of whatever is missing from or wrong with that cause, channel the emotion into coming up with clear goals to improve it.

Sharing your motivations with like-minded people can really boost a rebel spirit, too. What's more, the creativity and innovation of two minds is more powerful than of one.

Few roles in the business world demand a level of creativity more than copywriting. Michelle's ability to fly in the face of convention like a true rebel and come up with award-winning concepts for clients has stood her in good stead.

There was a time, however, when one of her ideas was so original that it was taken from her by one of her colleagues … a rebel without a clue!

Finding Her Sizzle

By Michelle Power

Senior Copywriter. I turn dull, complex and garbled messages into clear, compelling and engaging copy that builds brands and drives sales.
Newbury, United Kingdom

The cool quiet calm of the room was a blissful break from the humid noise and sticky urgency of outside.

Helen looked around her. The room was full of some of the biggest names of the day, funky glasses, hipster hair, loud designer clothes and louder opinions filled the beautiful Miami hotel ballroom.

On a long table, she sat amongst famous faces from the world of advertising. Dave Trott, writer, thinker and virtual advertising god. Rosie Arnold, famous not only being a brilliant creative and but for making it to the top, not just breaking but smashing a thumping great hole in the 'glass ceiling' and becoming executive creative director at one of the world's top agencies, all without compromising her femininity or being anything other than herself. And not ignoring Trevor Beattie, the man who'd brought the world Wonderbra's Hello Boys and saved a high street retailer with the company shorthand, FCUK, among many, many other award-winning campaigns.

She couldn't believe how far she'd come.

From little old Helen who'd have run a mile rather than even enter a room filled with these people, let alone add her opinion to the proceedings. The company was beyond daunting. Or it would have been, to the old Helen.

Her journey to this table had been a bumpy one in every sense of the word. From being called a 'lumpy bloke' in her first years working in advertising, through redundancies, promotions, awards, lows and highs.

But she didn't mind – she was just glad to have made it in an industry renowned for its being male dominated. Often, Helen and her creative partner, Alice, had been the only women in the creative department. But, as she kept hearing, things were different now. Not different enough, thought Helen.

Of course, it's not just the world that had changed. She'd come along way too.

Outwardly, she hadn't changed much; physically she was much the same, slim with a boyish build. Now, she had a far better clothes budget, making her uniform T-shirts and jeans a thing of the past. Thankfully.

But inwardly, she was very different. Just the fact that she was sitting there, with strong opinions and not terrified to speak her mind, spoke volumes.

"And last but not least..." called someone from the other end of the table.

Her attention was brought back into the room. The darkly decorated uber modern space with its architectural plants, deeply hued jungle print wallpaper and erratic art deco lighting.

At long last, the final campaign of a very long day appeared on the giant screen, ready for their judgement.

Taking a drink, Helen quenched her thirst, her mind was already starting to think about the ferry that was due to leave in just under an hour.

Putting the glass to one side she looked up at the screen. Suddenly everything stopped.

The room went silent.

Her heart stopped beating.

Everything and everyone vanished.

Her idea. She was looking at her idea. She couldn't believe it. All these years later and there it was.

And just as suddenly, here she is, sitting beside Alice on one of a pair of black leather sofas outside Dave's office. She's clutching an A3 presentation with what she and Alice excitedly believe is an award-winning campaign idea.

Opposite sits another pair of creatives, two men a year or two older, with their campaign idea lying casually, confidently even, on the coffee table between them.

She's in her twenties, not long out of art school, an advertising BA honours degree burning a hole in her parents' pride. She's the first person on either side of the family to go to university. A world of hope, opportunities and possibilities stretching out in front of her.

In advertising, 'creatives' as they were called, particularly those just starting their careers, are hired - and very often fired - as a pair, a team.

One is the copywriter, taking care of the words. The other the art director, taking care of the pictures. But most importantly in advertising, where the idea is king, both work together with often overlapping skills, to come up with the best, strongest, most memorable idea possible.

Alice and Helen are a great team. They make a good double act, bouncing ideas off each other, pushing, encouraging and challenging each other, their contrasting personalities working well. Alice the bubbly confident outgoing one, Helen the quiet one. Both determined in their own way.

It helps that they're friends as well as colleagues, as they're the only women in an all-male department.

But they have a problem. They're too modest, and yes, perhaps too female as well, to be the success they have the potential to be.

Dave's ready to see them now.

Helen and Alice go in first, leaving the lads waiting their turn on the sofa.

They place the TV story board, a series of pictures showing the key scenes in an advert, in front of Dave. Then step back silently, giving him time and space to read it.

He likes it. It's good.

He should like it. It's a great idea that has, as they say in the business, 'legs'. Dave can see the potential. He likes what he sees and better still, can see where it could go, imagining the ads not yet written.

This is beyond what they'd hoped for. Dave's suggesting future scenarios. This is brilliant. He can see the scope and opportunity, the 'big idea'. Their ideas are relevant, on brand, engaging. He can imagine them being repeated in the pub, a creative's dream.

This could be the start of a campaign, something big. Perhaps not quite "Meerkat" big, but big all the same.

They feel elated. It had all been worth it. All the hard work. The brainstorms that went on late into the evening. The weekends meeting up in the deserted office. The time they'd spent thinking as they went for walks with their other halves. In the bath. While falling asleep.

Coming up with ideas. Letting them live for a while before binning them, determined to find something better, stronger, more memorable.

It had all been worth it. Dave's reaction was beyond what they'd hoped for.

Floating out of Dave's office, they take their seats. It's the lads' turn now.

Helen and Alice aren't worried, it was a great presentation. Dave loves their work. He'd virtually said the shoot would be theirs.

The lads stroll confidently up to a smiling Dave, with the opening line, "You're going to love this Dave, we promise you, it's an award-winner!" With a flourish they push their work forward.

She can't believe her ears. How arrogant! Telling Dave what he'll think. Surely that will turn him right off. He won't like this one bit.

But he's laughing and they've not even shown him their idea. Now they're talking to him as he's reading it, telling him how well it works, how perfect it is for the client.

Surely, he's going to tell them to be quiet while he reads?

Hold on though, he doesn't mind at all. He's laughing. He loves it.

Helen and Alice sit silently looking at each other, unable to do anything more than just listen to what's happening.

Dave bought the lads' idea over theirs. It wasn't as good. But the confidence of their presentation had blown the girls' out of the water, even if the idea hadn't.

That was years ago.

A lot of water had gone under the bridge since then, they've moved agency, climbed the career ladder, created some great work.

Yet, even after all these years, she still knew in the pit of her stomach, with absolute unwavering confidence, ironically, that their idea had been better. Way, way better. And for once, she's confident that she's not being arrogant.

Turns out you can't always rely on something speaking for itself: you need to give it 'sizzle'. And the lads' had done this brilliantly, they'd given themselves and their idea sizzle and some.

But what the hell was 'sizzle', anyway?

Finding the answer to this was about to become a side job that would last for years. Something Helen was going to have to work at and, when she had money, invest in.

Realising her natural reticence and shyness were holding her back and hurting her chances of success, and that telling herself to "just snap out of it" wasn't working, Helen decided she needed to do something more.

Hypnotherapy. That should work. People could be made to do all sorts of things when they're hypnotised. Looking into it, low self-esteem and lack of confidence was a recurring theme with the surprisingly large number of local hypnotists. Perfect.

It wasn't cheap, but the investment would be so worthwhile. If it could break her lifelong lack of self-confidence, just imagine how much better life would be.

It turned out there was just one problem. The hypnotist was no match for her Olympian ability to worry. Putting someone under who is reclining stiff as a board worrying about everything that was, could or had happened, proved impossible.

That's okay. After the second visit when the hypnotist still hadn't been able to get her into a state of even mild relaxation, Helen had a brainwave.

A nip of vodka before the next session should do it.

It didn't.

The hypnotherapy was given up by mutual agreement.

Next there was 'Talking Therapies'.

The woman who conducted the sessions was lovely, but Helen couldn't help feeling they'd fallen at the first hurdle when it was decided her problem was being a perfectionist. She worried this was the wrong area to focus on. As the weeks went by, she worried nothing seemed to change. She worried she was wasting their time. She worried how much she was worrying.

This was probably how she'd been able to stay so slim all her life, while eating whatever she liked. For years putting on weight was one of the few things she didn't need to worry about. It turns out worrying burns a lot of calories.

Being a perfectionist wasn't the problem. Learning how to stop short or do a lesser job was never going to help.

She didn't know it then, but it was learning how to value what she did that would become the crux of her problem.

Everyone knows pride comes before a fall.

If you're proud of what you do and tell people you can do a good job, you're going to come a cropper.

It's true. Helen had come a cropper every time. It was a self-fulfilling prophecy. Pride always came before a fall.

The 'Talking Therapies' came to an end and life went on much as it had before.

Helen's career progressed. She was head-hunted for new roles which made her feel great. Initially. Before the worry set in as she tried to prove herself to a new line manager, team… world. Her work hours grew again, she started work earlier than everyone else, worked later than everyone else and did more weekends than everyone else.

But sometimes you just can't save yourself from yourself.

With yet another redundancy came time for Helen to try again and tackle her now crushing lack of self-esteem.

This time she spent what felt like a small fortune. In reality, it was just a rather large percentage of her now very modest income, on mindset coaching. It was a fantastic experience. She met some amazing people, heard incredibly insightful views and clarifying perspectives.

But somehow nothing stuck.

She'd heard the words, but she hadn't had enough belief or confidence to actually put what she'd heard into practise.

Was it Einstein who said, "Lunacy is doing the same thing again and again while hoping for a different outcome"? She couldn't remember, but whoever said it was right. And she was driving herself nuts.

Helen was good at what she did, she'd won awards, quite a few awards, some of them really big international awards.

So why did she have so little confidence?

Things came to a head when she set up her own business.

It was going to be her big opportunity, a chance to put all that energy, hard work and determination into building something for herself. She was going to go it alone. No looking for another job. She was going to become her own boss, and with the success that would hopefully follow, achieve her dream of travelling the world. Her other passion in life.

Helen gave her new business a name. Built a website and started networking.

An old friend became her first client, giving her bits and pieces of work - paid work that would benefit both of them.

She had her first paying client; she was up and running and felt great. Apart from one small, and very important area.

Money.

Putting a price on what she did caused her more anxiety than just about anything else. It was the same old problem, she didn't, couldn't put a value on her work. It felt like putting a value on herself.

Helen understood why people wanted a price up front. She would too.

So why did she struggle so much? Why was it that the number she came up with was so high? Was it high? She didn't really know.

If she could, she'd give her work away for free. Anything to avoid the painful subject of money.

It was time for more help. This time, with a brilliant salesman. A man who had once been down, picked himself up and built a hugely successful business. A man she'd heard talk, who made sense. His path hadn't been so different. Had it?

Putting her money where her mouth was one last time, she signed on the dotted line and soon found herself in a group of grown-up businesspeople.

Helen quickly realised she was out of her depth. These were people with proper businesses, who had staff, turnover in the millions. But they were lovely. And it turns out, they all had their own worries.

It quickly became apparent, nobody is really on top of everything, everyone has stuff going on.

So how could she get over her anxiety and boost her self-esteem?

Helen was asked to share a proposal, clearly her Achille's heel.

Putting a price on what she does. Only this time for a collective to comment on. Nightmare!

She immediately went into the familiar spiral. She'd calculate a fee, knowing it was a fair reflection of the time needed to do the work, and confident that it would make a significant difference to the client, really connect with their customers and help to boost business.

Then she'd falter. That seemed like such a lot of money. How could little old Helen really ask that much? It was way too much. Then she'd spend the same amount of time again trying to halve the fee.

Then she'd sleep on it.

Only, she wouldn't sleep.

In the morning she'd go over it again. Where could she cut it further? How could she halve it?

The worry would have a hold of her now.

What if they thought it was way over the odds? What if they thought, "Well, she rates herself pretty highly!" What if she didn't get it? Couldn't deliver? What if... What if... What if...

Helen wished she was in a position to do the work for free.

All this worry and it wasn't even a real proposal!

On reading the proposal, consensus was unanimous, and succinct. The fees were fine. Low if anything. But it lacked sizzle.

That word again.

After all these years Helen was still effectively placing her work on the table and shuffling back quietly, hoping the reader would see all in it that she could. That they'd have the vision to see what she could do, and the value she'd add.

It was time to stop playing at this. Helen had to get to the bottom of not only what 'sizzle' really meant, but how to find hers.

This time it would be different.

It had to. She was running out of time.

In the past she'd been told to think of a number and double it. Ha, ha - nice one. She was too busy trying to halve it.

She'd been told to take pride in her price. But how when she baulks at asking it?

She'd been told to pretend it wasn't she herself setting the fee, it was her finance department. A neat idea. But despite her years in advertising, she'd never been very good at lying – she needed to believe something to be convincing.

So how could she change?

Baby steps of belief.

She'd always been drawn to strong people and had been surprised and delighted when they seemed to like her, too. Perhaps it was time to stop dismissing them as just being kind, and start allowing herself to believe the encouraging, supportive things they said.

After all, she admired these people, it would be rude to dismiss them.

She'd taken her first baby step towards believing in herself.

Next Helen started working on ignoring her inner voice, the one that repeatedly told her she couldn't do it, she wasn't good enough, she was expecting too much.

It wasn't easy, and she couldn't ignore it for long.

But she did manage to ignore it for long enough to press send on a proposal and run.

The feedback was positive. A bit of negotiating, a slightly lower fee and she won the client.

So far, so good.

Next Helen asked some of her clients for feedback. What did they like about working with her? What could she improve on?

The feedback was enlightening. It turned out she'd helped her clients in ways she hadn't imagined. She'd given people who seemed to be completely self-assured the confidence they'd been missing.

She'd taken another baby step – she was believing the feedback.

She started putting this down in her proposal. Underplaying it at first. Nobody likes a brag.

After this she started adding small case studies of some of the things she'd done for her clients, things that showed what she could do. Importantly, with their testimonials.

It felt very braggy. Not her at all. But it wasn't her words, they were her clients' words.

It went down well. Yet another baby belief.

Then, she tried acting on another piece of advice she'd been given and ignored. Giving a price in a call. A ballpark figure of what the work would cost. This was torture. She'd always had great calls with potential clients, then hidden while she beat herself up about the price as she procrastinated drafting a proposal.

This time, she gave what she thought was a high number, then instead of bolting, held her breath. The voice at the other end of the line couldn't have been less phased by it.

Really? It had worked?

"Send me more information and examples of your work," was all that had been said.

Woohoo! Yet another baby belief in the bag.

With each nerve-wracking step she'd proven to herself, despite her conviction that it wouldn't, that it could actually work.

She was starting to believe it. Finally, she had proof.

Never one to accept things on face value, she'd had to prove it to herself before she could accept it.

And she'd finally proved it.

In the end, it turns out that for Helen, her sizzle eventually came from her believing that she was good at what she did. That she made a real difference to her clients. That her twenty-plus years of industry experience, combination of advertising and marketing and unique spin on things really did add value. They were no longer just words, she believed them.

It hadn't been easy to see it.

It had felt like bragging. But when she allowed herself to believe the evidence, she could repeat it and finally, she could put a number to it.

She could big up, with one hand firmly over her heart, the reasons why a client is brilliant and why their customers should buy from them. She just hadn't been able to do it for herself.

As soon as she learnt this lesson, the pieces fell into place. She quite literally hadn't looked back. Her career had taken off, her old advertising connections got back in touch. She was asked onto judging panels.

The noise in the hotel ballroom that had never gone away returned. The last campaign was under discussion, receiving praise and criticism. Generally, the consensus was positive. But when you get so many egos in one room, it was unlikely to ever be unanimous.

Looking at the work, Helen had a decision to make.

She could tell them it wasn't original. It was, in fact, the work of a young low-paid team who had never been recognised.

But this would mean trashing the reputations of the creatives whose names were attached to it now. It could sound like sour grapes. She may not be believed. Definitely, she'd need to find the proof and who knew where that was.

But most importantly of all, she'd really, really hurt two people she'd never met. For what?

She'd come so far. Achieved so much. Did she really need to do this?

But how had it happened? How had they entered her idea into an international award?

Was it possible it was just coincidence? After all, as the saying goes, there's nothing new in the world. The idea had come to her and Alice from somewhere. Maybe this team had got the idea independently from the same place – wherever that may be.

Checking the name of the agency, she quickly shelved that thought. Dave, her old Creative Director, was their Creative Director. Too much of a coincidence.

But even then, could it still be unintentional? Would Dave really have remembered it after all these years? If he had, would he then steer this team down the route of recreating it?

She wouldn't have thought so.

But then, she'd never have imagined it not being bought in the first place.

Her keen sense of right and wrong had been piqued.

Could she reveal the theft, claim the recognition that was rightfully hers and Alice's, and trash the work and the team?

She could vote for it. See her idea get the recognition she always believed it deserved.

To see it finally win a gong would be fantastic. Fair and well deserved.

Only it wouldn't be her name on the award.

It didn't take long for Helen to decide what to do.

Around the room discussions had ended and votes had been cast. People were looking to her now.

Speaking to nobody in particular she asked, "Is this the last one of the day?"

Murmurs of agreement combined a strong sense of relief with a palpable desire to get out of the room and into the bar.

Everyone was looking at her now. Willing her to give say her piece and for the judging to be finished for the day.

But things were worse than Helen had realised.

The vote was split. Everyone present thought it should get something. Some thought it should win the top gong, others just a recommendation.

The votes were so evenly split, Helen's vote would be the one to decide the fate of the campaign and the creative team behind it.

If they won the top gong, the black pencil, they could write their own cheques. Choose from the amazing job offers that would come their way. It would change their futures in ways they probably couldn't imagine.

If she called theft on the idea, the team's professionalism and reputation would be in tatters. Even in an industry that allows itself broad licence to borrow and be influenced, straightforward stealing was still not acceptable.

But when the dust had settled, she and Alice would finally get the recognition they deserved. Clearing her throat, Helen stood up.

"I'm afraid I have to declare myself unable to vote or even comment on this for personal and professional reasons."

The room groaned as one.

Old Helen would never have done this, to be cast into the spotlight like this, annoy so many people, it would have been unthinkable.

But she didn't need to be a people pleaser any longer. She'd managed to break that exhausting and thankless cycle.

"I realise this means you have no clear outcome and will need to vote again. I'm sorry, I know this is frustrating, but I'm afraid there's nothing I can do about it."

She'd walked away from things before, but not without a fight.

But this time was different. She was different.

She didn't need to trash anyone's career. She'd come a long way. Life was good. She loved the balance she'd found. Or should that be the balance she'd created. She was grateful for the opportunities that were coming her way, the lovely clients she was working with, the creative work she was producing, and the fact that she was finally earning enough to live the life she wanted.

With her head held high, more certain than she'd been of anything, she picked up her jacket and crash helmet and, ignoring the looks of dismay, strode from the room.

Crossing the gleaming hotel lobby, she headed out to the car park and her heavily laden Triumph Tiger. On the way, she made sure to generously tip the kind attendant who'd kept a close eye on her bike, ensuring nobody had been tempted to steal her baggage.

Without breaking stride, she threw a leg over the black leather seat, zipped her jacket closed, pulled her gloves on, and with more certainty than she'd felt in her life, pressed the ignition.

The bike roared into life.

Smiling, she looked about her, taking in the scene, knowing this would be a time she'd look back on.

Then she knocked the bike into gear and pulled away, heading for Miami Ferry Port and the boat that would take her to Cuba for her long-awaited adventure of a lifetime.

She'd found another belief, that she was happy with what she had. And she finally believed in herself, one hundred per cent. She had her sizzle.

It turned out that 'sizzle' was a surprisingly quiet yet reassuring feeling. One she liked.

Disclaimer: Not everything in this story is true. For starters, I'd never be able to get onto a Triumph Tiger, I'm very short and not used to riding yet, so I've got a little Benelli TNT 125. Other facts have been changed or invented too, either because the truth would be just too dull or because I wish what I've written was true.

Some names have also been changed, either to protect people's privacy, avoid embarrassing them, or so they can't give me a dead arm or sue me. The real people I have mentioned in no way endorse this story, and probably don't even know about it. If they do know about it, please know I have named you only out of admiration as you're some of the greatest people in advertising, people I wish I'd worked with or just enjoyed a drink and a chat with (Trevor – you're a hero and someone whose help will always be appreciated). Please don't sue me.

As for the award-winning ad, I could tell you what it was (there was one), but then I'd have to… no, I can't, I swore I'd never say.

As a greater writer than I once said, "I'm a writer, not a fighter". Most importantly of all, I really am finally on my way to finding my 'sizzle'.

To find out more: michelle@powerofwords.media
                      www.powerofwords.media

EPILOGUE

So, now it's your turn……

The following are the attributes we find in successful business people, the eight keys to success, if you like. You will find all of them written about by the authors in this book.

They are not the only qualities, but they are the most common, regardless of industry sector or country. They are universal across the planet.

Building all eight in our lives not only will transform your business, but it will also enhance your personal life too.

1. Facing the challenge – running away from key problems is avoiding the issue. Face the problem head on and handle it. Life is a series of challenges that will strengthen us over time, just like an athlete trains for a big event

2. Overcoming financial hurdles – this affects all of us, regardless of how much money we have. It's also a fundamental issue for most start-ups, who are cash-starved. There are creative ways to get over cashflow issues, whether it's for business or personally.

3. Openness to change – one of the common failings of business owners is to say, "I know that, this or the other …". They are blinkered. It gets worse as one gets older too. I'm part of the 'baby boomer' generation and we are referred to by Millennials as "beige Boomers." Whilst we might have great experience, we don't have all the answers. Learning from the insightful input of others is crucial to business growth.

4. Will to accept help from others – It sometimes goes against the grain to accept help. It might feel that we are weak and vulnerable. The reverse is true. I've grown so much with the input of others over the years and have done things I never considered doing before. Looking at a problem in a very different way has been the repeated outcome from my enlisting the help and support of others. Even just receiving wise counsel on an issue over a coffee and can be uplifting. You can't get that from an email or a meme!

5. Adapting our view of life – I thought I knew it all in my 20s and 30s. I found out that I didn't. Mt view of Life and what really matters has changed, for the better. But the process of getting there hasn't been easy. It's challenged my perception and some of my values. As they say, every day is a school day.

6. Courage – one of the killers of a business is indecision. Having the courage to follow a plan is essential. It might be refined as time goes on, but the decision to act in the first place is critical. Dithering and lack of action starve the business of much needed oxygen. Even if a plan turns out to be the wrong one, have the courage to change it.

7. Single-mindedness / tenacity – just go for it. Life is short, go with your idea one hundred per cent with passion and dogged determination to make it work. Yes, take the wisdom of others, but go with your gut feel and instinct.

8. Desire to beat the system – successful business owners often swim against the current against perceived wisdom. Wanting to carve out a new way of doing things is fundamental to innovation and creativity. After all, it will give you a distinct USP from your competitors. Be a market leader, not a follower.

The chart on the next page is for you to mark yourself 1-10 (10 being the highest) against each of the 8 keys for success. Then do the same with your family, staff and clients, to gain an average - a basic 360-degree feedback.

Get them to be honest. People tend to give a 7 out of 10 as a default. You don't want that. You want honesty from yourself and honesty from them for this to be of value to you.

It's a way of identifying the areas you should focus on going forward, so that you can develop your business and yourself.

If you feel you need some help along the way, get in touch with me by DM on LinkedIn at linkedin.com/in/robgoddard

Most importantly, don't forget to have some fun doing this. You only have one life, so make the very most of it and enjoy everything it has to offer!

The keys to success	Self	Family	Staff	Client	Av. score
1. Facing the challenge					
2. Overcoming financial hurdles					
3. Openness to change					
4. Willing to accept support from others					
5. Adapting our view of life					
6. Courage					
7. Single-mindedness/tenacity					
8. Desire to beat the system					

Printed in Great Britain
by Amazon